ERIC NEWBY was born in London in 1919 and was educated at St Paul's School. In 1938 he joined the four-masted Finnish barque *Moshulu* as an apprentice and sailed in the last Grain Race from Australia to Europe by way of Cape Horn. During the Second World War he served in the Black Watch and Special Boat Section, and was a prisoner-of-war from 1942 to 1945. After the war, his world expanded still further – into the fashion business and book publishing. Whatever else he was doing, he always travelled on a grand scale, either under his own steam or as Travel Editor of the *Observer*.

BY THE SAME AUTHOR

The Last Grain Race
A Short Walk in the Hindu Kush
Slowly down the Ganges
Love and War in the Apennines
On the Shores of the Mediterranean
Round Ireland in Low Gear

ERIC NEWBY

A Small Place in Italy

LONELY PLANET PUBLICATIONS

Melbourne • Oakland • London

A Small Place in Italy

Published by Lonely Planet Publications
    Head Office: 90 Maribyrnong Street, Footscray, Vic 3011, Australia
                       Locked Bag 1, Footscray, Vic 3011, Australia
    Branches: 150 Linden Street, Oakland, CA 94607, USA
                       2nd floor, 186 City Road, London, EC1V 2NT, UK

First published 1994 by HarperCollins Publishers
First US edition published 1998 by Lonely Planet Publications, by
arrangement with HarperCollins Publishers Ltd
This US edition published 2008 by Lonely Planet Publications

Printed by The Bookmaker International Ltd
Printed in China

Author photograph by Wanda Newby

National Library of Australia Cataloguing in Publication Data

Newby, Eric, 1919-2006 .

A small place in Italy.

ISBN 978 1 74179 529 5.

1. Newby, Eric, 1919-2006 – Homes and haunts – Italy –
Massa-Carrara (Province). 2. Authors, English –
20th century – Biography. 3. Massa-Carrara
(Italy: Province) – Social life and customs. I. Title.

945.540926092

Text © Eric Newby 1994
Map © Lonely Planet 2008

LONELY PLANET and the Lonely Planet logo are trade marks of Lonely
Planet Publications Pty. Ltd.

To all our friends at I Castagni
whom we will never forget

Acknowledgements

To Wanda and Sonia who
remembered so many things that I had forgotten,
to Lucinda McNeile and Rebecca Lloyd at HarperCollins
and Hazel Orme at Picador for all their help.

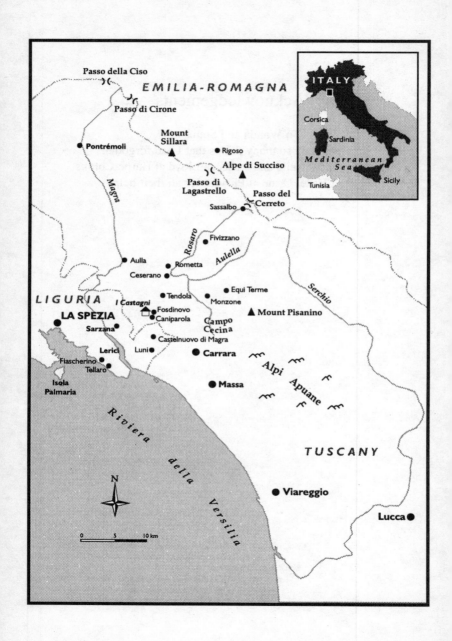

My dear little house
you were not there before
but in a short time you have grown
like a flower.
I beg you to remain
beautiful
and not to lose your colour.
I am about to go
because I have
a call from far away
but I will carry you
in my heart
for eternity.
Goodbye my little house.
Goodbye happiness.

Giuseppe Tarsiero, 1981

Chapter One

IN AUGUST 1942, whilst serving with the SBS, I was captured during a raid on a German airfield in Sicily, a year before the Allied landing took place.

In September 1943 the Italian armistice was announced and the following day, on 9 September, together with all the other inmates of the camp in the Po Valley near Parma, I absconded in order to avoid being sent to Germany, as did thousands of other prisoners-of-war in camps all over Italy.

The one thing that most of these escaping prisoners had in common in the course of the succeeding months was the unstinting help they were given by all sorts and conditions of Italians who risked their lives in doing so without any thought of subsequent reward. One of these, a girl called Wanda, subsequently became my wife.

Once out beyond the barbed wire, which up to that time had effectively insulated me and my fellow prisoners from the country and its inhabitants, and after I had been transported high into the Apennines, I found myself in a little world inhabited by mountain people whose way of life was of another century. A world in which there were few roads, scarcely any machinery of a labour-saving kind, one in which everything connected with working the land was accomplished with the aid of mules, cows and bullocks. Even wheeled vehicles were only of limited use. In these mountains the most common method of transportation was wooden sledges. It was a world in which when the snow came the inhabitants were cut off for long periods of time. Living with these people I gradually began to understand their way of life and their closely knit society.

But not for long. In January 1944 I was re-captured by one of the armed bands of Fascist Milizia, supporters of Mussolini's puppet republic of Salò, which continued to function until he himself was captured and shot during the last days of the war in Italy in 1945. From Italy I was sent to Moosburg, a vast prison camp in the marshlands near Munich, then to a place in what had been Czechoslovakia but was now Silesia, which the Germans called Märisch Trübau, what the Czechs had known in happier days as Moravská Trebová. From here, after a series of terrible events which resulted in the deaths of two officers, we were moved *en masse* to a camp near Braunschweig in western Germany where finally, on 14 April 1945, 2400 of us were liberated by the Americans.

At the end of 1945 I managed to get to Italy where Wanda was already working for an organization known as MI9 whose job, now that peace had come, was to seek out and help civilians who had helped escaping prisoners-of-war. Once again I found myself, and this time with Wanda, entering into the world of the *contadini* in the Apennines above Parma which by now I had grown to know so well.

In 1946 we were married in Florence, and ever since that time we have continued to visit the people who helped me all those years ago.

✜

While I was a prisoner in Germany I thought constantly of a day when the two of us might be able to return to the mountains and buy a house of the sort I had been hidden in and lived in while I was on the run. In February 1945, one of the last few awful months of the war in Germany, I wrote in my diary, imagining such a house:

It is an evening in late November. Outside the wind has risen, tearing through the trees about the house, bringing rain drumming against the window panes. The lamp is out and the fire casts enormous shadows on the ceiling and on the bookshelves, lined with much-read books.

Then suddenly, the wind dies and the rain ceases. The silence by contrast is enormous. Look now into the heart of the fire where slipping logs have formed strange caverns. Will I then remember the life in the prison camps: the damp blue fog that hung about those now far-off barrack rooms in which we seemed entombed, far into the day; the sudden, senseless arguments in which we all participated; the air-raid sirens wailing day after day, night after night; the bombs from the Fortresses, the Lancasters, the Wellingtons and the Mosquitoes streaming earthwards in their thousands to where we crouched, hemmed in by the all-embracing wire which allowed no escape; the long evenings when, from seven o'clock onwards, we sat around a flickering margarine lamp. Shall I remember these things?

I can remember them, all these things. That is if I want to. But I prefer to think of the friends I made, both British and Italian, their courage in adversity, and I thank God that we were not prisoners of the Japanese.

For the memory is selective and it is easier to remember what one wants to remember, so if I have to choose between the splendours and miseries, I will choose the moments of happiness in spite of the fact that there are few situations in which men and women are completely happy and completely free.

We both of us dreamt of buying a small house in Italy, one in which we might be able to re-create the happiness we both remembered; but it was not until more than twenty years after the war ended that we found ourselves in a position to realize this ambition.

What follows is the story of how we finally succeeded in doing so, and of the whole new world of friends and acquaintances we found on the way.

Chapter Two

IN THE AUTUMN of 1967 I went to Africa to visit the game reserves, then the latest craze, and write about lions who took siestas in trees, and other wonders, as Travel Editor of the *Observer*.

While I was there Wanda sent me an express letter from Italy which somehow contrived to arrive in a couple of weeks when a month was around par for a letter from there whether it was sent express or not.

In it my Slovenian, who likes to keep things stirred and on the boil, wrote that what she had feared was now beginning to come to pass. The prices for houses anywhere near the sea in northern Italy were beginning to go up and it would only be a short time before houses in the depth of the countryside would follow suit. 'Unless we do something quickly we shan't be able to buy anything at all,' she concluded on an appropriately pessimistic Slavonic note.

Spurred into action by this *cri* I flew from Africa to Italy instead of back to London and eventually came to a halt in a place called Tellaro, where Wanda was staying in a tower, originally built as a lookout against roving Saracenic pirates who used to come ashore on these Mediterranean coasts in search of livestock for the north African harems.

This tower was the property of Wanda's friend, Valeria, with whom she had worked in 1943. Tellaro is near Lerici on the shores of the Ligurian Sea, at the mouth of the Gulf of Spezia, where Byron went for a six-mile swim. At that time (in 1967) it was still a fishing village, an almost unbelievably picturesque one, that looked as if it had been designed by Rex Whistler, and it was still inhabited by fishermen sufficiently genuine to roll out of bed every morning at 4 a.m., except Sundays, or even earlier, and put to sea, making a hideous din.

In summer a cool breeze blew up from the sea through Tellaro's dark and cavernous streets, filling the gleaming white bed sheets that were drying on the lines stretched high overhead between the opposing houses as if they were spinnakers that were drawing nicely. But not always. When the *scirocco*, a nasty wind from Africa, blew, bringing torrential rain, thunder and lightning along with it, what had been magical, mysterious caverns became deep, dank ditches full of water, then Tellaro was not so *allegro*.

For Tellaro and a number of similar places on the shores of the Mediterranean, that autumn was the beginning of what was soon to be a period of extraordinarily rapid change and transition.

One moment Tellaro was a fishing village with a few artists hidden away in it; the next it had been 'discovered' by senior people in Fiat and Olivetti and suchlike organizations, who saw it as an ideal place in which to immure their wives and families during the long Italian summer, less boring than Forte dei Marmi. A place to which they could drive down from Turin or Ivrea, or wherever it was, on Friday evenings in a couple of hours or so, driving back on Sunday nights to the embraces of those of their mistresses who could stand August in such places as Turin or Ivrea, or wherever it was they were returning to.

Within a year or two smart little fish restaurants would be springing up around Tellaro's minute piazza, opened by locals who soon became 'characters', the sort who treat their clientele with carefully cultivated insolence, a sort of treatment the rich and powerful, rather surprisingly, seem to enjoy, turning them into suppliants.

And in a couple of years or so most of them would have either grown rich by selling their houses or plots of land, or else, more modestly contented, would be doing well working in the bars and restaurants, and in the souvenir and picture postcard shops.

A member of one of these local families, by this time very elderly, whom we happened to meet, was a still sprightly lady who had known D. H. Lawrence and Frieda von Richthofen. They had come to live in Italy in September 1913, returning in July 1914 to England, where they were married. In Italy they rented a house in a small seaside hamlet between Tellaro and Lerici called Fiascherino. Every day this *signora*, then a young *signorina*, used to walk along the coast path through the olive groves to Fiascherino, where she used to do the Lawrences' housework and sometimes the cooking.

'I called him Signor Lawrence,' she said, the 'ce' as a soft 'che'. 'He was very thin and he had a beard. He looked as I imagined *Gesù* would look. And he enjoyed the wine.'

'Signor Lawrence,' the Signora said, 'had a wife. She was a German, a *nobildonna*. She was *simpatica*. Then, suddenly,' she said, 'they went away. We didn't know where.

'One of the things they left behind them was a big trunk full of papers and a key to it. They never came back for it. There was no money in it, only papers.

'Then, one day, I can't remember when exactly, a *signore*, a foreigner, I think he was an American, came to our house, I was married then, and said that he was a friend of Lawrence and that he had been given permission to take some papers from the trunk, so I let him do so.

'Then, one day, many years later, another *signore* appeared, also a foreigner. He said that Lawrence was dead and he, too, took papers from the trunk, all that remained.

'You may think I was stupid to let them have these papers,' she said, 'but they were all written in English or German and there was no one at that time in Tellaro who could understand them. The words were difficult words.'

The Signora lived in La Canonica, The Presbytery, a fine old house in Tellaro, in an apartment on an upper floor. She wanted us to buy it because, she said, she liked us; but for us it was too high up and too dark. Also it had no garden, not even a balcony or a terrace to sit out on. So we didn't buy it. But when we told her that we couldn't buy it she cried a little and then gave us as a parting gift two silver spoons with the arms of the von Richthofen family engraved on them.

Inspired by all this we began to look for our house as soon as I arrived from Africa. It soon became obvious that it was not going to be easy. What had up to then looked like desirable properties immediately ceased to do so when we began to look at them more closely.

It took ages to locate most of them. Sometimes we felt like travellers in a desert in which the mirage was operating. What looked like a desirable place at a distance ended up by being perfectly awful when we actually got to it, or else, as with a genuine mirage, unfindable, a figment of the imagination. Some were nice but too near the road, some had no outlook, some had outlooks, but very gruesome ones, some were too ruined, too lonely, too frequented, too noisy or too expensive.

We soon decided to abandon completely the search for anything near the sea. Neither of us had wanted to be near it, anyway. The only reason for being near it was that it would have been nice to have found a place near Tellaro, where Valeria and her husband lived.

We got an introduction to a surveyor, a Signor Anselmo. He was tall and slim and nice to talk to and he lived in an apartment block in Lerici. Surveyors seemed to us to have enviable lives. All they did was to tell their customers that the places of their dreams were riddled with dry rot, or were built on the lines of geological faults and were likely to disappear into the bowels of the earth without warning. 'You may think you need a surveyor,' an American resident in Lerici told us, 'but you need one like you need an attack of the hives.'

No, Signor Anselmo didn't know of any property that would suit us down here on the coast. He advised us to go inland, even a few kilometres inland. Inland it was different, he said, but it was outside the area in which he operated. He did, however, know someone who might be able to help us, a Signor Vescovo who owned a *bar/ristorante*. Signor Anselmo kindly offered to telephone him.

Later that morning we presented ourselves at Signor Vescovo's *bar/ristorante*. Signor Vescovo was smallish, slightly rotund, aged between forty and fifty and wore thick, tortoiseshell glasses. Was it his name, Vescovo, which means bishop, that invested him with a faintly priestly air?

He, himself, as he told us, was in the process of selling his business and was at present engaged in negotiating the purchase of a large farmhouse somewhere near a place called Fosdinovo, across the river Magra in the foothills of the Apuan Alps, which he was proposing to convert into a *ristorante* specializing in wedding receptions and anniversaries, in which the food on offer would be what is known in Italy as *produzione propria* (home produced). According to Signor Anselmo, Signor Vescovo knew more about the buying and selling of properties in this particular area than anyone else.

'There is one house that I think you would like very much,' he said as we drank a coffee with him. 'It is on the side of the hill just above the place where I am trying to buy the farm. It is rather ruined and it only has about two thousand square metres of land but it is a pretty place and very quiet. It belongs to a Signor Botti, a *contadino* who lives at a place called Caniparola, a small village at the foot of the hill. I think he might be persuaded to sell it as it doesn't render anything except a bit of wine and a small amount of olive oil; but like all *contadini* he needs time to make up his mind.

'If you would like to see it,' he went on, 'I can arrange it for this afternoon. I will send a message to the Signora who has the key to it by the local bus, telling her that you will come at whatever time you say. I will also write down the instructions about how to get to the house which is called I Castagni [the 'I' pronounced as in 'E'] – The Chestnuts.

'And if you are wondering why I am not going to charge you anything, even if you buy the place, it is because I owe a favour to Signor Anselmo.'

Chapter Three

AFTER ONCE MORE becoming imbrangled in the labyrinthine one-way street system of Lerici, we followed Signor Vescovo's painstakingly written instructions about how to get to I Castagni, and crossed the river Magra by a long, multi-arched, brick bridge. Below it, strung out along its gravel banks, a number of despairing-looking men were fishing without apparent success as they, or their descendants, continued to do for all the years we lived in the area.

Beyond the river we followed the Via Aurelia, one of Italy's more dangerous roads, to Sarzana, an ancient, walled town on the borders of Tuscany. Here we entered the Plain of Luni, the site of what had been Luna, an important Etruscan city and seaport which Livy described as being 'the first city of Etruria' and Strabo as having one of the finest and largest harbours in the world, much of its prosperity being because of the marble trade.

But in the fourth century AD its decline began, brought on by the malaria which eventually rendered it more or less uninhabitable. It was subsequently sacked many times: by the Lombards, by the Normans in the ninth century and by the Arabs, who finally destroyed it and carried its inhabitants into captivity in 1016. Both city and seaport disappeared from history some time in the twelfth century, killed off by the malarial mosquitoes, and became an area largely populated by ghosts and goats. Now all that remained of it was an amphitheatre that once seated six thousand spectators and a theatre. It was Luna that gave its name to what is now the present region of Lunigiana, although originally it was much larger.

Then, after a couple of miles, we turned off on to a minor road at a place called Ponte Isolone, a hamlet on the Via Aurelia made up of some half a dozen buildings which included a café, a seed merchant, an ironmonger's and a shoe shop, all of which, except for the shoe shop, which never had anything in our sizes, we subsequently patronized.

Once on this minor road the roar of traffic on the Via Aurelia became a faint murmur and we found ourselves, as if by magic, in rural Italy. It led away, dead straight in a northerly direction, to where the foothills of the Apuan Alps rose steeply from the plain. Rising above them, deep blue in the distance, were their big peaks, the highest of which, Monte Pisanino, is 1945 metres high, with what looked like snow fields on their flanks. These were the *ravaneti*, great screes of glistening white marble, debris from the quarries above Carrara.

We had, in fact, although we didn't know it at the time, left Liguria at Ponte Isolone and were now in Tuscany, in the province of Massa Carrara, a narrow strip of it not much more than a mile wide, salient with the road running up the middle of it and with Liguria on either hand. High on the hillside there was a long-abandoned customs house, on what had been a frontier.

Here, on what was good, alluvial farmland, olives and vines and maize and wheat flourished, and in the lower parts of the foothills lived what had been *mezzadri*, crop sharers, dependants of the ancient Malaspina family, who at one time had enormous possessions. The family owned the towns of Carrara and Massa Carrara until the middle of the eighteenth century and had a palace and a castle in the latter, and another castle in Fosdinovo up on the hill in the direction we were now going, which was acquired in 1340 by Spinetta Malaspina. Other rich landowners also had *mezzadri*, who originally gave half their produce to the landowner in exchange for the use of the land and their dwellings, but by the 1960s they received 58 per cent of the proceeds. Those employed by the Malaspina used to live in humble and, by the standards of the time in which they were built, decent, now picturesque farm buildings, many of them built as late as the 1900s by the Conte Malaspina, as a marble plaque displayed in a prominent position on the outer walls of each of them testified.

The majority of these, and the other farm buildings, were rendered in the standard colour for Italian farmhouses almost everywhere except the mountains, known as *sangue di bue* (ox-blood), which grows paler and paler as the years pass until it ends up a very pale pink.

Many of these *mezzadri* had begun to work on the land when they left school at the age of eleven after five years of *scuola elementare*, an educational system that endured until the last war. At the time when we bought I Castagni in 1967, the *mezzadria* system was still functioning in some parts of Italy and there were still numbers of *contadini* who were more or less, if not totally, illiterate, and could only make a cross on paper instead of writing their names. Today, most of the occupants of the farmhouses are salaried agricultural workers.

Now we were passing a vast and beautiful villa, also rendered in *sangue di bue*, built by the Malaspina in the eighteenth century at Caniparola, a comparative rarity in what had always been, since the coming of the malaria, and until the development of the Riviera della Versilia in the second half of the nineteenth century, a poverty-stricken part of Tuscany.

It was not only the malaria that the inhabitants had to contend with. Besides having to put up with the already mentioned Saracenic pirates who whisked their womenfolk away, they had to endure being trampled underfoot by an almost endless procession of foreign armies, which used what was a much-trodden route over the Apennines from the valley of the Po and then down the valley of the Magra, on their way south to despoil Rome and other attractive places *en route*.

What the natives in these northern parts of Tuscany needed to survive such irruptions were not villas but castles, the more Gormenghastian the better, preferably situated on inaccessible crags, and such fortresses were built in considerable numbers.

Because of this comparatively few purely domestic villas were built where we now found ourselves. Here, at Caniparola, the hamlet near which the Malaspina villa stood, the road ran past a little chapel, embellished with marble obelisks, in which the family used to attend mass when they were in residence, and passed under an imposing brick archway, part of what had been a huge stable block. The lower parts of the building were plastered with posters announcing incredibly boring decrees, printed in full, or what was going on with the local pop groups. It was a great year for pop, 1967, the year of Sergeant Pepper.

Having passed under the archway, unless the road had made two violent turns, first to the left, then to the right, we would have run straight into the façade of what was to prove to be a rather good, very rustic inn, the Trattoria all'Arco.

Because of this man-made hazard the driver of almost every vehicle ascending or descending the hill, when confronted with it, felt constrained to sound his horn, what for a late twentieth-century Italian was the equivalent of crossing himself, at the same time going into a screaming gear change.

If the vehicle happened to be a bus, one of the service which operated between Sarzana and Fosdinovo, then the sound of the horn at close quarters was unbelievable. It was therefore not surprising that the Arco was a rather noisy place at which to eat in the open air.

Beyond it the road began to climb the hillside – at that time Caniparola was a very small place with no modern buildings at all, apart from one or two post-First World War ones – winding its way upwards in a series of hair-pin bends, through fields planted with vines and olives, passing old farmhouses all painted in various shades of *sangue di bue*.

As we climbed we began to have fleeting views of other places, such as Castelnuovo di Magra, a hill town across the valley to the right which had a castle rising above it. Confronted with what seemed an endless succession of these bends, all of them more or less identical, with what looked like identical vineyards and olive groves sandwiched between them, we began to wonder if we had passed the track which led to the house we had come to see; but on this matter Signor Vescovo's instructions had been explicit, and we would have had to be barmy to make a hash of them.

'After a farmhouse on the left of the road with a vineyard in front of it in which the vines are supported on stone columns, the only such ones in the zone, you come to the seventeenth bend.

'Beyond this,' he continued, 'you pass on your right a food shop, a butcher's shop and a communist cell with a hammer and sickle over it.' (This was a branch of the Italian Communist Party which, by that time, had passed the peak of the popularity it had enjoyed in the 1950s and early 1960s, epitomized in Guareschi's *Piccolo Mondo di Don Camillo*.) But in spite of it now being closed, probably for ever, we always called it 'The Cell' because it sounded more exciting than a branch.

'Then, after the eighteenth bend, you will see, a hundred metres or so up the hill, a tall solitary cypress, from which a rough track leads off to the left.

'This track,' he wrote, 'leads down to a small house. In it lives a widow, a Signora Angiolina. She has the keys of the property and she is expecting you at three o'clock.'

All the years we subsequently lived here we had trouble with what Signor Vescovo described as the eighteenth bend from Caniparola. Wanda made it the twenty-second, I made it the twenty-first and none of the friends who came to stay with us was able to agree how many there were either. It was a waste of time appealing to the local inhabitants, they had never even attempted to count them.

✝

Signora Angiolina was hovering in her vegetable patch outside her house, awaiting our arrival. As she told us, she had just finished feeding her rabbits which lived in a large wooden hutch at the back of the house.

The house looked bigger than it really was as she had rented a large room on the ground floor to a communist social club which was, at the moment, like the cell at the seventeenth bend, more or less moribund, but not completely so, and subsequently it started up with evenings of very un-communist pop which would have made Lenin turn in his grave.

Signora Angiolina's husband had died a couple of years previously and because of this she was in deep mourning, which meant that she was dressed in black from head to foot: black headscarf, black cardigan, black skirt, reaching below the knee, black woollen stockings – normally she wouldn't have worn any at all before the cold weather set in – and black felt slippers.

The only item that wasn't black was her apron which was dark navy with small white spots on it, which helped to cheer her outfit up a bit.

Later she told Wanda that she was fed up with being in mourning – the navy apron was probably a first sign of rebellion against it – and she was looking forward to leaving it off and quite soon she did so, which raised her spirits no end.

Signora Angiolina was in her sixties when we first met her, and was very slim. She had nice, bright-blue eyes and she cried easily. She had greyish-brown hair drawn back tightly from her forehead in a bun, now hidden by her headscarf. And she had a really lovely smile.

It was a tragic face but a beautiful one, a beauty, one felt, that would endure and in fact it did, until the day she died. Even seeing her briefly for the first time it was obvious that at some time in her life something awful had befallen her but we had to wait until we were on more intimate terms with her in order to discover what it was.

Like most *contadini* she was wary of people such as ourselves who came from cities and were foreigners but, in spite of this, she did bestow on us this lovely smile.

However, when Wanda asked her if she would take us to see the house and unlock the doors for us so that we could see the inside, which was the purpose of our visit, she suddenly looked serious, shrugged her shoulders in a way that was almost imperceptible, and said, '*Ma!*'

This seemed like bad news. In my experience almost all the Italian *contadini* I had ever met who used this expression had done so in a negative sense, one that usually boded ill.

When, for instance, while on the run in Italy during the war, I had asked the *contadini* for whom I was working in exchange for food and a roof over my head, if I had any chance of remaining free when the snow fell in the Apennines, something I had been thinking about for some time, there was no doubt as to what they meant when they said, '*Ma!*' They meant 'No!' And they were right. But Signora Angiolina's '*Ma!*' was of a different sort. One she used in the sense of '*Chissa?*' ('Who knows?')

But this was not her only interpretation of '*Ma!*' If you asked Signora Angiolina, '*Che sarà successo?*' ('What can have happened?'), a question that we would be asking all and sundry in this part of rural Italy for the next twenty years or more, one which could cover any sort of calamity – a blow-back in a septic tank, the sudden disappearance of the roof, or the cessation of the water supply – her first reaction would be to say '*Ma!*', implying that she didn't know.

What she meant by '*Ma!*' in this particular instance, as Wanda subsequently explained to me, being more practised in the understanding of such things, was that she was not the actual owner of the keys, and was therefore expressing trepidation at the thought of having to be responsible for opening doors to rooms to which she may not have had access previously, unless someone had died in one of them, in which case she might have entered it for the wake.

Worst of all, for her, was the idea of opening them up for a couple of unknown persons who might quite easily turn out to be robbers. But in spite of all this, the implication was that she would do it. It was all rather confusing.

Her other favourite expression, one which she used when confronted with a *fait accompli* which had on the whole turned out well, as, for example, if I had cut down, as I subsequently did, one of two trees, and it turned out to be the right one I had felled, not the wrong one, was '*Hai fatto bene!*' ('You have done well!'), uttered in resounding tones.

I loved it when Signora Angiolina gave me one of her '*Hai fatto bene!*' broadsides. It always gave me the feeling that I had just received an accolade from the Queen for saving her corgis from being run over, or that I had just been kissed on both cheeks by General de Gaulle after having been decorated with the Croix de Guerre avec Palmes for doing something frightfully brave and important – 'Well done, Eric!'

In fact if Signora Angiolina called me anything it was what everyone else called me in this part of the world, that is if they called me anything, which was 'Hayrick' without the 'H', 'Eyrick', or failing that 'Enrico'.

So now, having delivered her '*Ma!*', Signora Angiolina went off to get the keys from some hiding place, five of them altogether, all very old, three of them large and very beautiful works of art.

Then, having armed herself with a small reaping hook and giving it a preliminary sharpening on a special sort of sharpening tool embedded in a large log, she set off down the track, leading the way, to the place where Signor Vescovo had written that there was a way to the right off the main track. From this point it then made a very steep, slippery descent to a little bridge which, at that point, spanned a torrent.

'The track goes down through a chestnut wood,' he had written, 'which is why the houses and the place are known as I Castagni.'

The bridge which spanned the torrent was nothing but a couple of cement drain pipes covered with earth. The torrent itself was deep, narrow, bone dry and almost completely hidden from view by the chestnut trees which soared up into the air from the ravine the stream had carved for itself. The bed of the stream was horrible, filled with the refuse that people further up the hill had chucked into it: bits of plastic sheeting, half buried in the bottom of it, empty bleach containers, rusty tins and other assorted muck.

Now, for the first time, we saw the house.

It stood at the far end of a grassy dell, overlooking the terraced fields that covered the hillside one above the other, and it was surrounded by vines and old olive trees that cast a dappled shade as their branches moved in a light breeze from the west.

The house itself faced south. It was sheltered from all the winds that blew between north-east and south-east by the groves of chestnuts that also rendered it invisible from further up the hillside in summer, and did so even now in what was autumn although the leaves were beginning to thin out.

It was a small, two-storey farmhouse, built of stone partially rendered with a cement that, over the years, had turned a creamy colour in some places and in others a lichenous green. The overall effect was of a building on the verge of becoming a ruin.

It was roughly rectangular in shape, roughly because it was possible to see where, over the years, other small wings had been added on, which was why the ones that looked the oldest were roofed with stone slabs. Others, of more recent date, were covered with tiles that had either weathered to a faded pink, or else to a yellowish golden colour. To prevent them being whisked away by some freak wind, stones the size and shape of footballs were disposed along their outer edges in what looked like a rather dangerous fashion for anyone standing below if one of them rolled off.

There were no roses, or any other kind of climbing plant winding their ways up the walls, as there would have been in England. No garden. No shrubs, only an orange tree. There was no muck lying about either, apart from that in the torrent. Everything else was spotless. This had been up to now a strictly utilitarian establishment.

As soon as we had taken all this in, without even seeing the interior, we both knew that this was the house we had been looking for and this was the house we would have to have if we were going to have one at all.

The first door we came to had the orange tree growing up a wall to one side of it. As was all the other timber used in the construction of the house – floorboards, roof timbers and joists – the door was chestnut.

The planks from which this had been made had faded over

the years to a beautiful silver-grey colour but when Signora Angiolina finally succeeded in turning the key in the lock and we went inside, the door shut on us and we found ourselves in what would have been complete darkness, if the door had not been riddled with holes through which the sun shone in long, slender beams as if someone had fired a shotgun at it.

Yet although it looked as if it was on its last legs, as did the bridge over the torrent, and one of the first things that would have to be replaced if we bought the house, this door was still there, in the same condition, when we finally left I Castagni twenty-five years later.

What we were now standing in was a room about fifteen feet long, ten feet wide and six feet high, what had been a cowshed, or a stable for mules, or possibly both.

Until very recently the principal means of moving supplies from one place to another in the mountainous areas of Italy had been by pack mules, hand carts, big wooden sledges with sides made of wattle, wooden stakes interwoven with split branches, which were usually drawn by cows. For the rest it was what people could carry on their backs.

A few years before we arrived on the scene the asphalt road up which we had driven, following the bends, had not existed. Neither had the bends. All there had been in those days was a steep, cobbled mule track which went straight up the hill from Caniparola to Fosdinovo without any bends at all, and stretches of this ancient route still existed and were still used by local people travelling on foot.

The floor of the cowshed was also cobbled, with thin rectangular stones laid edge to edge. Iron rings for tethering the animals were sunk in the rough stone walls in the back part and there was still a good deal of dung lying about, but so dry and powdery that it was impossible to know what sort of animal had produced it.

The only illumination, apart from that provided by the self-closing door with the holes in it, which was of rather limited usefulness, came from a small, barred window that looked out towards the bridge over the torrent some thirty yards away.

Overhead a trap door with a ladder opened up into a room which had been a hay loft. It was almost twice the height of the cowshed and much brighter, the light entering it through a large opening in one of the walls through which the hay had been forked up. Other illumination was provided by gaps in the tiled roof where the rain had been coming in. Every bit of timber in these two rooms – beams, ceiling joists and floorboards – was riddled with wormholes and you could break off bits as if they were biscuits.

Further investigation was made impossible because someone had had the truly devilish idea of more or less filling the loft with large coils of heavy wire, of the sort used to set up trellises in vineyards, each of which was inextricably interlaced one with another. The only other way in was round the back of the house where there was another door, literally in mid-air, which needed a ladder to get to it.

Meanwhile, as we were taking in all this ruin, lizards, no doubt deluded by the mild November weather into thinking spring had come, or it was still summer, scuttled about upside down on the tiled roof through which daylight was only too clearly visible. Looking at it I felt that one of us would only have to emit one really hefty sneeze to bring the whole lot, beams, floorboards, joists, roof tiles and all, down about our ears. On one beam there was the skin cast by an adder. Every year, even when the beams were put in order, the adder or its descendants continued to shed its skin in this same place.

'*Ma,*' said Signora Angiolina, as we all three gazed at these irrefutable evidences of decay. What she meant by this enigmatic utterance, devoid of the usual exclamation mark and without the shrugging of the shoulders, was not clear, although I could hazard a guess. It was the first observation she had made since we reached the house, though she had made it abundantly obvious that she was not happy about the condition of the torrent when we came to it. '*Sono gente ignorante,*' she said, but to whom she was referring was not clear. It could have been a whole band of ignorant people.

'Cor!' I said, the English equivalent of Signora Angiolina's epithet. If the first two rooms were like this what on earth would the others be like?

Only Wanda expressed herself clearly and confidently, although she had said, 'My God!' when she first saw the loft and its roof; but then she had recovered.

'Providing Signor Botti doesn't want the earth, we'll be all right,' she said.

Having exhausted the possibilities of the cowshed and the loft for the time being, we moved on westwards to the main door of the house, passing on the way a bread oven that was built into the wall with a brick chimney rising above it to the height of the upper storey. According to Signora Angiolina it was out of action and was likely to remain so. The only man capable of repairing it had contracted a painful skin disease of a sort that repairers of ovens and users of cement are apparently liable to and was unable to carry out any more work of this sort.

To the right of the door a flight of stone steps led to the upper floor where the chimney of the oven terminated. Originally these steps had been protected from the elements to some extent by a tiled roof but the main support of it, a long beam, had collapsed, taking all the tiles with it and smashing most of them.

High overhead the main chimney stack rose into the air. It had a flat stone on top of it, supported by four rough brick columns, each about a foot high, to stop it smoking. To me it looked more like a tabernacle of the Israelites than a chimney.

Now we waited outside the front door while Signora Angiolina, Mistress of the Ceremonies, a role she enjoyed much more than being in mourning, selected the right key to open it. This was the finest door in the house. In fact, although rough and primitive, it was one of the best of its kind in the entire neighbourhood, apart from those we saw in some houses up the hill in Fosdinovo, but those were doors of town houses rather than rustic ones. It was difficult to imagine one more rustic than ours. Subconsciously, we were already beginning to refer to objects such as the doors at I Castagni as 'ours'.

This door consisted of a number of large slabs, probably cut from a single tree and set up horizontally, one above the other, on a stout frame. These slabs were of a beautiful dark colour and looked as if they had been soaked in oil. And this is what we later discovered they had been treated with, linseed oil over a long period, a treatment which we ourselves were to continue.

Such a door would have been irreplaceable if it had been damaged and every time we came back to the house from England our preoccupation was always with the door. Had it fallen to pieces? Had it been damaged by vandals? These were the questions we always used to ask ourselves while descending the hill and crossing the torrent. In fact, like most other objects at I Castagni which we took over, it outlasted us.

The key for this door, which, like all the others, was of hand-forged iron, was the biggest of the lot. It was a key that was easily identifiable, even in the dark, not only because it was the biggest but because someone at one time had attempted to turn it in the lock, or perhaps another lock, and when it had failed to open had inserted a metal rod through the ring at the end of the shaft and twisted that a full half turn without breaking it. Now, in order to turn the key in the lock, it had to be inserted upside down and then jiggled about for what could be ages. Yet we never considered the possibility of changing the key and the lock for a new one. The key was much too beautiful. In fact there was another complete set of keys but I lost them the first day we took over the house and we never found them again.

This lock had the peculiar foible that when the wind was blowing from the south-west it would open itself. The only way to prevent this happening was to secure the door to a ring-bolt in the outer wall of the building using the wire of which there were great coils in the loft.

This door opened into a living room of an unimaginably primitive kind, with a floor made from rough, irregular stone slabs on which it was difficult to set a chair without it wobbling.

To the left, as we went in, there was an old, varnished wood, glass-fronted cupboard with blue-check curtains, an *armadio a muro*; and against the far wall there was something known as a *madia*, of which this was a very ancient example, a kneading trough for making pasta with a removable top, which could also be used as a table.

To the right of the door there was a *fornello a carbone*, a charcoal-burning stove, built of brick, and next to it was an open fireplace, with a shelf over it. At one time, what must have been a long time ago, the walls, the stove and the fireplace had all been white-washed but by now the smoke of innumerable fires had dyed them all a uniform bronze colour.

Inside the fireplace a long chain extended up the chimney into the darkness from which was suspended a large copper pot, and round about the fireplace were disposed a number of cooking utensils, all of them archaic but all of them still in use. The ashes in the fireplace were fresh and there was plenty of kindling and enough logs to make another fire stacked to one side of it.

The other furniture, all of it apparently homemade, consisted of a small table with a plate, a bowl and a knife, fork and spoon set on it, a chair and a minute stool that looked as if it had been made for a child, for sitting in front of the fire. But although they were homemade these items had been constructed and repaired with great skill by whoever had undertaken the work.

The only window was small and barred with metal slats, like the one in the cowshed. Beneath it there was a small marble sink with a brass tap that was working; above it was an extremely dangerous-looking electric light fitting, which consisted of a bulb connected to the two naked wires which supported it by a couple of blobs of solder, a lighting system that was not at that moment working, although Signora Angiolina said she knew how to get it going.

The only other illumination was provided by several small, homemade brass lamps, fuelled with olive oil, that looked as if they might have been looted from an Etruscan tomb.

'Who has been living here?' Wanda asked Signora Angiolina. This was the first intimation we had had that someone might already be in residence at I Castagni.

'This is the room,' Signora Angiolina said, with a certain air of surprise, as if this was something that was common knowledge, 'in which Attilio lives.'

'But who is this Attilio?' Wanda asked. By the way she spoke I knew that she was worried. Neither of us had envisaged the existence of a sitting tenant or, even worse, a squatter.

'Attilio is the brother of the wife of Signor Botti, the *padrone*, the owner. He is only a little man,' she said, referring to him as an *ometto* – as if his smallness was some sort of recommendation. '*Ma lui è molto bravo.* He knows how to do everything.'

What we had already been forced to designate mentally as 'Attilio's Room' – were we really going to have him as a sitting tenant, even though he was '*molto bravo*'? – was separated from the back part of the premises by a partition made from *canniccio* – wattle and daub. *Canniccio* was made with interwoven canes, the thinnest of the giant reeds that grow everywhere in this part of the world, plastered with a mixture of clay, lime, dung and chopped straw. These reeds, which grow to a great height, fifteen feet or more, were everywhere on the hillside and once established spread like wildfire. Their roots had the consistency of cast iron and in trying to eradicate them I succeeded in bending a pick.

These canes had dozens of uses: as supports for clothes lines, for supporting vines and making pergolas, for fencing in earth closets and rendering the user invisible to the vulgar gaze, for picking fruit from tall trees (by attaching a little net to the end of one of them). And when they finally rotted and broke they made good kindling. Meanwhile, unless ruthlessly controlled, they devastated the countryside.

Now the whole of this partition wall was riddled with woodworm and was beginning to fall apart. A ruinous door in its left hand side opened into what had been another cowshed. It was difficult to imagine domestic animals, however domesticated, walking through one's kitchen/living room on their way in from the fields in the evening to their sleeping quarters and each morning going the other way, back into the open air, but this was presumably what had happened.

This cowshed was also cobbled. It was also completely windowless. These downstairs rooms were so dark that I began to wonder if the inhabitants had been spiritualists. What was good news was that the floorboards overhead and the beams that supported them were in quite good condition.

The key that opened the door of the room at the top of the outside staircase was the most complex and beautiful of all the keys and the easiest to use. There was no juggling or jiggling necessary. The Signora inserted it the right way up and it opened first time.

Inside there were two rooms, back and front, divided from one another by a less ruinous version of the partition wall on the ground floor but reinforced with wooden uprights that gave it a slightly olde-Englishe, half-timbered appearance. To the left of it, another rickety, lockless door, similar to the one on the ground floor, separated the two rooms, front and back, both of which had two windows. All four were minute. It was obvious that if we were going to be able to read in either one of them, even in broad daylight, we would have to have bigger windows and these walls would take some excavating as all of them were composed of large stones and were more than two feet thick.

The roof itself appeared to be more or less sound but the main beam which supported it, a really hefty piece of chestnut, would have been more reassuring if it hadn't had a great crack in it.

Looking at it, as I already had at numerous other beams and boards during this tour of inspection, I found it difficult to decide whether I Castagni might be good for another hundred years, or might collapse altogether in the course of the next couple of hours.

The view from the outside balcony of this upper floor was terrific. Here we were about eight hundred feet above the sea. It was a beautiful afternoon and the sun shone from a cloudless sky, flooding the front of the house with a brilliant golden light.

To the west, beyond the house, the grassy track that led past the front of it from the torrent, gradually descended a hundred yards or so beyond it between lines of vines to a pretty two-storeyed building, a smaller version of I Castagni; and some fifteen miles or so beyond it were the mountains of the Cinque Terre beyond La Spezia, behind which the sun was now beginning to sink, like a huge orange.

Far below to the south-west was the Plain of Luni, with its innumerable small holdings and market gardens. And beyond them were the wooded heights that rose steeply above the far, right bank of the Magra, here running down through its final reach before entering the Ligurian Sea.

It was at this moment that I took a black-and-white photograph of the house which, when it was printed, had more of the quality of an engraving than a photograph, a magical effect, but one that I was never able to emulate, however hard I tried.

Down on the ground floor, at the foot of the outside staircase, next to the front door and at right angles to it, there was another door that opened into what was a miniature, protruding wing of the house. This part of it was almost completely severed from the main part of the building by a frightful fissure that ran from top to bottom of it.

According to Signora Angiolina, who had been living in the neighbourhood when it occurred, it had been caused by the great earthquake of 1921, which had damaged or destroyed a number of houses in the region. Again I had the feeling that yet another part of the building might be about to collapse.

This was the only room in the house to which Signora Angiolina did not have a key, apart from the one that opened the door to the loft at the back of the house, the one that was going to need a ladder to get to it.

The only way one could see into this little room was through a heavily barred window; fortunately the wooden shutters were open.

It was a very small room, freshly whitewashed and lit by the same sort of oil lamps we had seen in the kitchen. The few bits of furniture, which almost completely filled it, consisted of a large, old single bed of polished wood with a high back inlaid with mother-of-pearl; made up with clean white linen sheets which were turned back, ready to receive whoever was going to sleep between them. Alongside the bed there was a little stool covered with a worn fragment of carpet, and on the wall next to the bed there was a crucifix and an oleograph of La Santissima Vergine del Rosario di Fontanellato, Wanda's village near Parma, where I had been a prisoner-of-war in 1943, and below it there was a small, circular, marble-topped table, which it later transpired contained a *vaso da notte*, a chamber pot.

On the other side of the bed there was a very old wooden chest. Overhead the whitewashed ceiling looked decidedly wonky, with big patches of damp where the rain had penetrated; but in spite of this the room was a lap of luxury compared with the rest of the house, and the only part remotely ready for occupation.

'And who sleeps in this room?' Wanda asked superfluously. Like me she already knew the answer before Signora Angiolina confirmed that this was the bedchamber of Attilio. It was also unnecessary to ask who washed and ironed his sheets. '*Sta arrivando adesso,* Attilio,' she said. 'He is coming now.'

Chapter Four

EMERGING FROM the deep shadow cast by the trees on the banks of the torrent we could see a small figure travelling towards us across the grass at a tremendous rate, rather like one of those *gompa lamas* who move across the Tibetan plateau at high speed, negotiating what would seem to be impossible obstacles on the way. A method of progression made possible only because they are in a trance state.

Soon we could see him clearly. A tiny, wizened man, bent by a lifetime of toil, toothless so that in profile his mouth looked like a new moon. He was old, how old it was impossible to say, anything between seventy and eighty, quite possibly even more.

As he drew near we could hear him talking to himself in an animated way, and occasionally laughing at some private joke. He was certainly nothing like a *gompa lama*, more like a benevolent gnome.

He was dressed in a pale-coloured jacket, baggy trousers, a white, open-necked shirt and on his head he wore a big, pale-coloured cap that looked a bit like an unbaked sponge cake. Everything about him was very clean looking.

Now he was abreast of us and I prepared to welcome him, or for him to welcome Signora Angiolina, or welcome the three of us. But he did none of these things. Instead, he looked at us benevolently, cackled a bit while fishing a modest sized key from a pocket, said something that sounded like '*Bisogna vedere un po*'', the equivalent of 'I'll have to think this out a bit', then

37

opened the door to 'Attilio's Bedroom', took the key out of the lock and went in and shut the door, still continuing to chuckle away on the other side of it.

I was completely bowled over by this encounter. I was sure I had met him before on two occasions in 1943, after the German occupation of Italy.

The man I remembered had looked more or less the same age and that was twenty-four years ago. Then I had thought of him as being very old, I suppose because anyone over the age of forty looks old when you yourself are twenty-four. And I remembered that he had already lost his teeth which had made him look older than perhaps he was.

The first time had been at the end of September when he had been the mysterious third man in the car decorated with a red cross in which an heroic Italian doctor had been driving me to the Apennines along the Via Emilia, what was then the main German line of communication with the battle front to the south. In Parma, which was stiff with Germans, the car, a Fiat propelled by gas, had broken down in Piazza Garibaldi, the main square of the city. There we had been surrounded by German *Feldgendarmen* armed with Schmeisser machine pistols telling us to hurry up with our repairs and be gone. While the doctor and I had been trying to get it going Attilio, if that was who he was, had sat in the back seat, dressed in a garment called a *tabar*, a voluminous cloak, cackling away at them completely unafraid.

The second meeting I had with this mystery man was later that winter when he literally saved my life after I had become hopelessly lost in a thick forest and got soaked to the skin in a river. He had put me up for the night in what must have been one of the loneliest houses in the Apennines. The front door of that house was almost exactly the same as the one here, at I Castagni. I wondered if it reminded him of it too.

It was Attilio (or was it?) who, later that same evening in the house in the mountains, told me the extraordinary story of what happened after Maestro Giovanni shot the Bird with the Golden Wings and gave it to the King; and it was he, the following morning, who put me on the right track back to the cave in which I had been living, and from which I had strayed like a lost sheep.

But it was impossible that he and Attilio could be the same man, if for no other reason than that of age. The man I had known in the autumn of 1943 must have been long since dead.

'What we've got to do, before we buy the house, is to talk to him,' Wanda said; but trying to interview Attilio proved to be like trying to interview a will o' the wisp.

✝

As we went up the hill with Signora Angiolina we had a last, fleeting glimpse of the little house through a break in the trees. Smoke was coming from the chimney which meant that Attilio had emerged from his place of refuge in the bedroom and was about to start preparing his evening meal. I wondered what it would be: perhaps some magic potion that would render him invisible.

A little later, sitting in Signora Angiolina's cavern-like kitchen, eating cake and drinking the white wine made with long-ripened grapes, of a sort that was always produced for honoured guests, she told us what she knew about Attilio. We, ourselves, decided to say nothing.

'Attilio is a very good little man, *un ometto molto bravo,*' was how she described him for the second time that afternoon, as though we hadn't taken it in. 'He can do anything, repair anything, make anything. Some people think he is a bit strange, because he talks to himself more than he does to other people but he does this because he is really rather *timido* and some people make fun of him.

'When he was young,' she went on, 'he learned the work of a blacksmith, and of a wheelwright. He can still work anything in iron or wood and he can make spades and hoes and the handles for scythes and for any other tools that are needed.

'And he can make ladders, the triangular sort called *tramalli,* and he makes the oil lamps you saw in the kitchen.

'Once he made a merry-go-round for the children hereabouts, and paid for a band to play while he made it turn.

'He also made a cinema in which you looked through a sort of telescope [what she probably meant was a magic lantern] at coloured pictures, while a gramophone played music.

'He even made an aeroplane and launched it with him inside it from a high place on the way to Fosdinovo, but the machine fell to the ground and he was injured. He doesn't like to be reminded of this.

'But his greatest skill, because he has such a good memory, is as what we call a *narratore di fiabe*, a teller of tales. Attilio inherited this skill from his father, who learned it from his father. There were also women who told stories, *narratrice*, they were called.

'He knows many stories, Attilio – *L'Uomo Verde d'Alghe* (The Green Seaweed Man), *L'Uomo che Usciva Solo di Notte* (The Man who Only Went Out at Night), *L'Oca con le Penne* (The Goose with the Feathers), *Il Drago e la Cavallina Bianca* (The Dragon and the Little White Mare), and many, many more. Some are very old, from the time of the *Saraceni*.'

I knew. I had already heard whoever the old man in the mountains was tell two of his stories, the one about *Maestro Giovanni*, the other *Il Figliolo del Re Portoghese* (The Son of the King of Portugal) back in 1943, in the course of the second of which, being very tired, I had fallen asleep, but when I woke up he was still telling it.

'Now,' said Signora Angiolina, 'Attilio is the last *narratore* in these parts and when he goes that will be the end of the *fiabe*.'

'He is also very religious,' she went on. 'And however difficult things are for him, he never complains,' she concluded. 'The other night it began to rain very heavily and I was worried about him. So I went down the hill to the house – he was already in bed – but there was a light shining through a hole in one of the shutters covering the window of his bedroom. I looked through it and there he was, sitting up in bed reading his breviary with his umbrella open while the rain came pouring through the ceiling. The next morning he went up on the roof and repaired it.

'Of course I didn't tell him about seeing him in bed with his umbrella. He would not have liked it.'

With what, in card-playing circles, amounted to a full house, it seemed unlikely that Attilio was in any imminent danger of losing his *pied à terre*, at least not for some time. Somehow we were going to have to reconstruct the house around him, as if he were an Emperor in a Ming Tomb.

Chapter Five

A S SOON AS WE got back on the Via Aurelia we telephoned Signor Vescovo and told him that we would like to buy the property and asked him how much the owner, Signor Botti, wanted for it. We didn't dare use the telephone at the shop or down the hill at the Arco at Caniparola. If we had done so the news of what was happening would probably have been broadcast over the entire neighbourhood.

'He isn't asking anything at the moment,' Signor Vescovo said. 'As I already told you he hasn't yet made up his mind whether to sell or not.' Signor Vescovo was not the sort of man who liked having to repeat himself and he was repeating himself now. 'If he does decide to sell,' he told me, 'the price will be, two and a half million', which was then the equivalent of about £1500.

'Will he take less do you think?' Wanda asked, who dearly loves a struggle.

'I think,' said Signor Vescovo, 'that the price is not negotiable.'

'How long do you think it will take him to make up his mind?' I asked, being of an impatient disposition.

'It is difficult to say. It could be any time. The only thing you can do now is to wait. When he does decide I will let you know and then you must come instantly in case he changes his mind. And you must bring the money. You may have to pay in ready cash. It is probable that he may not know anything about cheques. I don't think it's wise to bother him with such matters. They would only upset him.'

'Where do we get two and a half million in cash?' I asked Wanda when she hung up.

'Don't worry, we'll get it,' she said.

'You're in the wrong business, stringing along with a writer, a sorry scribe,' I said.

'I know,' said Wanda, 'you're doing your best.'

I was thinking about Signor Botti and Attilio, and tried to imagine either of them with a cheque book and a current account at the Monte dei Paschi di Siena, Sarzana Branch, but failed.

The following day, cutting what had been our holiday short, we drove 900 miles to Le Havre and caught the midnight boat to Portsmouth. If we were going to have any time at all at I Castagni, that is if we succeeded in buying it, which we were both set on doing, then I was going to have to hoard any holidays owed to me like a miser.

✛

Some three weeks later we received a telegram from Signor Vescovo. The message consisted of four words: '*Vieni subito prezzi lievitano*', 'Come instantly prices rising', in the sense that dough rises.

Two days later we set off on the road back.

By now the weather had deteriorated dramatically. There was snow at the mouths of the Mont Blanc Tunnel on both the French and Italian sides and when we reached I Castagni rain was falling steadily with occasional violent gusts of wind from seawards.

The subsequent meeting eventually led to us becoming the owners of what, in the prevailing conditions, contrived to look a somewhat less attractive property than it had done formerly. It took place, not as we imagined it would, indoors in the kitchen out of the way of the elements, but on an exposed piece of high ground at the rear of the premises from which a fine view could be obtained of its various ruined rooftops, with the rain belting down on them.

Other amenities, of which we had so far been ignorant, included a well lined with masonry which subsequent sounding proved to be about fifty feet deep, and a very rickety lavatory (in this case an outside earth closet without a roof) with a seat so small that it must have been hewn out by Attilio for his own personal use. It hung over what appeared to be a bottomless rift in the earth's surface.

I knew a good deal about this sort of lavatory, fenced in by *canniccio*. They give whoever is seated within an entirely false impression that he or she is invisible to those in the world outside. During the war in Italy I had helped to rescue a buxom *contadina* named Dolores from a similar one in the Apennines, when the seat on which she had been perched had given way, precipitating her into its unspeakable depths, and a very unpleasant job it had been getting her out.

Present on this historic occasion were Signor Botti, the vendor – or was he going to be a non-starter? – and Wanda and myself, the buyers. Signor Vescovo was to act the part of *mediatore*, intermediary or mediator for the deal. Without the intervention of a *mediatore* no deal could be concluded, and in many places still cannot be concluded, in rural Italy, whether it involved the sale of a flock of sheep or the construction of some unsightly building for which no planning permission existed.

Signor Botti was a man of about sixty-five. He was very thin and had a long, melancholy face which rarely, if ever, betrayed any emotion, a face hewn by a Mayan from some dark, brownish stone. He had been involved in a terrible accident when one of his legs had been run over by a tractor, which had left it in the shape of a bow. He was obviously in constant pain but endured it with great fortitude.

He spoke to us in what was an almost completely unintelligible dialect, which even Wanda, who could understand but not speak Parmigiano, the dialect of the Province of Parma on the other side of the Apennines, could make little of. It was fortunate that Signor Vescovo was fluent in it.

Signor Botti's rather grim appearance belied his nature which was that of a nice, rather timid man who was not very well off and was, with good reason, terrified of being taken for a ride by two foreigners over what was, almost certainly, his most valuable asset.

He was dressed in a dark brown suit and a waistcoat with a heavy, silver watch chain draped across it, a white shirt without a tie, a snuff-coloured felt hat and mountain boots.

For this meeting all four of us had elected to bring umbrellas; and there we stood with them straining to turn themselves inside out while the rain hissed down, the lightning flashed and the thunder rolled and reverberated in the marble quarries above Carrara and recurrent blasts of what was the *scirocco* from Africa endeavoured to remove us from the hillside. Why this meeting had to take place in the open air in such apocalyptic conditions remained unclear, until Signor Botti proceeded to march us round the boundaries of the property, which were identified by small stones almost invisible to any but the most practised eye, rather like the choirboys who once a year beat the bounds of the Church of St Clement Danes.

But this was not the end of it. He then took us on a conducted tour of the various interior parts of the house, all of them, in order, as he said, that we should be absolutely sure that what we were getting was what he was selling.

'That is,' he said, looking thoroughly pessimistic, 'if we are able to conclude something,' which, at this moment, seemed highly improbable.

This second conducted tour led to the discovery of an amazing room at the back of the premises, at the far end, yet another part of the domain of Attilio. It was a room roofed with stone slabs and it had a door which could be only opened by inserting a hand in a hole in a wall and groping around until you could grasp a baulk of timber which acted as a lock, and pull it from left to right.

This room extended the whole height of the building and had originally been constructed for the purpose of drying chestnuts. They were laid out and dried over a fire that had a chimney which extended up to the height of the roof. When they were dry they were ground into a pale, brownish flour and used to make a rather sickly, sweetish sort of bread called *castagnaccia* which, until long after the last war, was a staple food in many parts of mountain Italy.

It contained a great collection of tools, a forge with bellows, several ladders, a couple of wine barrels, rather the worse for wear, some of the heavy tubs called *bigonci*, from which the grapes were poured into the grape crusher, various agricultural instruments, wooden mousetraps that looked like miniature lock-up garages and were fitted with a sort of portcullis made of tin that would come down on the necks of the unfortunate mice if they tripped the trigger, axes, hammers, crowbars, scythes and sickles, leather clogs with wooden soles, boxes of hand-forged iron nails and racks of empty wine bottles of ancient manufacture, very heavy and black – all this to enumerate just some of the contents. Miraculously, it was as dry as a bone.

And even after all these preliminaries, getting Signor Botti up to the starting line, so far as selling his house was concerned, was about as easy as bringing a reluctant bride to the altar. Although he had, apparently, agreed to accept two and a half million, which was what he asked for in the first place, he was not going to do so before the whole business had been gone over again with Signor Vescovo.

There followed what turned out to be an entire hour of rumbling, rambling dialogue conducted between Signor Botti who, I regret to say, I was beginning to have a desire to strangle, notwithstanding his disability, and Signor Vescovo whom we were both beginning to admire profoundly for his almost inhuman self-control. In the course of these exchanges Signor Botti, rather like the Grand Old Duke of York, at one moment advanced to take up a certain position, the next retreated from it, then advanced again to re-possess himself of it, while we all got wetter and wetter, having re-emerged for no apparent reason into the open air.

Then, suddenly, their dialogue ceased and Signor Vescovo seized Signor Botti's right hand, at the same time contriving to bring our two right hands together with his, with the words, '*Dunque, siamo d'accordo!*'

It was done. At least we thought it was done. Nothing was as I had imagined it would be: no repairing to some snug hostelry, such as the Arco, for drinks all round, while we dried out. Only the four of us on an only too convincing Italian equivalent of a blasted heath. No sign of Attilio, whom I would not have been at all surprised to find lying in state in his bedroom, waiting for the weather to improve, or for that matter of Signora Angiolina, either.

What became only too apparent immediately, and something that put an additional damper on the proceedings, was that, as Signor Vescovo had predicted, Signor Botti didn't like the look of Wanda's cheque, or rather it was Wanda's mother's (she was paying for it), one little bit.

He took it gingerly in both hands as if it might have been about to explode and after holding it up to what light there was, getting it nice and damp in the process, and generally behaving as if it was something the cat had brought in, rejected it.

We were in a spot. We needed the money in cash, not next week or the week after, but now, if we were going to be sure of getting I Castagni. If we didn't produce it Signor Botti might quite likely succumb to another attack of the dithers and we would be back where we came in.

It was at this moment that Signor Vescovo who, so far as we were concerned, was getting nothing out of all this, showed himself worthy of his name and offered to cash a cheque himself for two and a half million and give the money to Signor Botti, which we didn't want him to do.

But first there had to be a meeting with Signor Botti's notary in Sarzana to finalize everything.

So we all tramped across the bridge over the torrent which was in spate, up the hill past Signora Angiolina's place in the hissing rain, from which she waved encouragingly when we gave her the thumbs up sign, piled into the Land Rover and set off for Sarzana.

There in the office of the notary in the main square, we were told that a declaration would have to be made that Wanda was the only surviving child of her parents' marriage. She was, in fact by now, the only survivor of a family of eleven children, only two of whom, Wanda and an elder brother, had survived beyond birth.

To do this we would have to go to Monfalcone, near Trieste, where Wanda's mother's notary carried on his business and would do what was necessary.

We took a night train to Monfalcone, got the document, spent the next night with Wanda's mother, got the money in cash and returned to find that Signor Vescovo had already come up with the money and handed it over to Signor Botti.

Now, apart from a few formalities, we were the owners of a small place in Italy called I Castagni.

Chapter Six

THE WINTER THAT followed our acquisition of I Castagni was a bitter one. Our house, which was near Wimbledon Common, was colder than most, due to the fact that we hadn't been able to afford to have central heating installed. All our resources had been consumed in stemming a disastrous outbreak of dry rot which had necessitated the removal of the entire façade of the building, so that while repairs were being carried out, looking at it from outside, having lifted the tarpaulin which covered it, was like peering into a doll's house.

Sometimes, when working at home on some piece for the *Observer* with a title such as 'The Best Bistros in Martinique', written by someone I had commissioned who complained of the heat in the Caribbean, to restore my circulation, long before jogging was invented, I used to go running on Wimbledon Common and across Richmond Park.

There, while pounding up the long snowy rides in the dusk, between the giant oaks that had been planted centuries ago, with the rooks like black rags scattering on the wind high above them, I thought of the little house in Italy, as full of holes as the sieve in which the Jumblies put to sea, and Attilio, its diminutive occupant, and wondered if they were both still standing. The house was not even insured. In the excitement we had forgotten to insure it. Should we now be thinking of insuring Attilio, in case the house collapsed on top of him?

One thing was certain: no one except Signor Vescovo, and he

had his own troubles what with his *ristorante* and his *produzione propria*, or our friend Valeria at Tellaro would think of letting us know if anything untoward happened.

The only other persons even faintly interested would be Signora Angiolina and Attilio and all that one was likely to get out of him would be a series of 'Heh! Heh! Heh!' noises, which was what it sounded like when he went through the motions of chuckling to himself, while Signora Angiolina's contribution would probably be a '*Ma!*'

All we could do now was to wait until the following Easter when, all being well, I would be able to have some more time off in which we could take possession of our newly acquired property. It was fortunate that by this time our children were sufficiently grown up to be at universities and no longer reliant on us for amusement during the holidays.

✛

Easter Sunday fell almost as late as it possibly could, and when we set off for Italy on the Tuesday of Easter week, it was in a Land Rover crammed with everything we could think of that might help us to survive in what was little more than the shell of a house.

All the way across France and Northern Italy it poured and poured, except at the Mont Blanc Tunnel where it was snowing at both ends, as it had been the previous time. As Wanda said, 'When it comes to travelling we are some pickers!'

We eventually reached the eighteenth, twenty-first or twenty-second bend, or whatever it was, in the early afternoon of Good Friday, Venerdì Santo. The weather was much too bad to attempt to open up the house and we decided to stay the night in a hotel up at Fosdinovo. We had had enough of camping.

So we continued on up another lot of bends until we reached the town of Fosdinovo, which up to now we had not seen except once in passing through it, and there we put up at one of the two hotels.

The town was situated on a steep-sided spur, more than 500 metres above the sea, and much of it was almost completely hidden from view behind its mediaeval walls and ramparts. The hotel we had chosen to stay in stood just outside the lower of the two principal gates. To the east and west the ramparts terminated in a series of precipices, falling away on the eastern side to dense forests. To the west they fell, equally steeply, to the same sort of terraced hill country in which I Castagni was situated. Through it ran a deep gorge, carved out by a torrent that had its origin higher up the mountainside, and eventually emptied itself, that is when there was any water to empty, into the Magra near Sarzana. All in all, Fosdinovo would have been a difficult place for a besieging army to take. The only possible way would have been to attack it from the top of the spur but this was effectively defended by the vast Castello Malaspina.

The Castello was an ideal residence for the Malaspina who spent much of the time over many centuries, in common with other members of the local aristocracy, plotting. From the fourteenth century onwards, they were a power in the region, reinforced by judicious couplings with such famous families as the Gambacorti of Pisa, the Doria, the Centurione, the Pallavicini of Genoa, the Orsucci of Lucca, the Santelli of Pesaro and the Cangrande della Scala, a union recorded by a marble relief over the entrance to the Castello, depicting a dog with a flowering hawthorn in its mouth. And they remained a power until 1796 when Carlo Emanuele Malaspina was deprived of his domains by the French.

The hotel was of a sort that had already long since become a rarity in most parts of Italy, even the most remote, and although we neither of us knew it at the time, its days in its present form were numbered.

Old, if not ancient, dark, cavernous, rambling were just some of the epithets that could be applied to it without being offensive. In fact it was lovely. Its rooms were full of good rustic furniture of the mid-nineteenth century and of later date, of a sort that we would have been only too happy to acquire for I Castagni: presses and chests-of-drawers in mahogany and chestnut which could swallow up heaps of clothes; cylindrical marble-topped bedside tables of the sort that Attilio possessed which also secreted within them massive *vasi da notte* with floral embellishments, receptacles of which, judging by the sanitary arrangements obtaining at I Castagni, we were going to stand in constant need.

But most desirable of all were the beautiful bedsteads, of all shapes and sizes, built of wood or wrought iron with tin-plate panels painted with flowers and arcadian landscapes, or decorated with mother-of-pearl, or very simple ones constructed entirely of wrought iron with no embellishment at all.

The hotel was owned by a local butcher who had a shop a few yards up the road, inside what had been one of the gates of the town. He also made excellent *salami*. He was a good butcher, but he always gave the impression of being on the point of falling asleep, like the Dormouse in *Alice in Wonderland*. Even shaking hands with him was an enervating experience.

His wife was of an entirely different disposition: large but not fat, black-haired, full of energy, what the Italians call *slancio*, and with a voice that made the rafters ring, and she was as adept at cutting meat or boning hams as her husband.

She was also extremely generous. The morning of Easter Saturday when we left the hotel to go down to I Castagni and paid our bill she gave us an entire *salame* as if it were an arrival present, and whenever thereafter we bought anything in the shop and she was there she always gave us something extra, which meant that we couldn't use it as much as we might otherwise have done.

There were two daughters of marriageable age, both of whom had fiancés. They were personable girls and were a good catch for any young men, with an hotel, a *ristorante*, a *caffè/bar* and butcher's shop as visible future assets. Meanwhile they acted as waitresses and chambermaids and ran the bar, all of which was enough to be getting on with, while the Signora's elderly mother did the cooking for the *ristorante* with some outside help in the season, which had not yet begun. Both subsequently married.

After we had signed in and had been consigned to one of the cavernous bedrooms which by now, with the awful weather prevailing outside, was almost totally dark, the two girls invited us to take part in the *Processione del Venerdì Santo*.

This procession, which had to end in the afternoon, at the hour of Christ's death, was due to start in a couple of minutes from the Oratorio dei Bianchi, an old church in the middle of the town. In the course of this procession the participants would make an almost complete tour of it. They themselves were going to take part. Would we like to go with them? We said yes.

Swathed in the warmest clothes we had at our disposal, but still inadequately clad – the wind was coming straight off the Apuan Alps, which were newly snow-covered – we set off with the girls for the piazza in which the Oratorio was situated and in which the procession would be assembling.

The piazza was about the size of a squash court and one side of it was entirely taken up by one façade of the Oratorio, an austere and beautiful construction of what appeared to be almost translucent marble. It had been built in 1600 by Pasquale Malaspina and a great marble escutcheon over the entrance displayed the coat of arms of the Malaspina, a flowering hawthorn. Below it there was an Annunciation carved in the same material. Inside the building, hidden behind the high altar, was a wooden statue of the Madonna, carved in 1300 and lodged here when the church was built, after the original one was destroyed by fire.

Normally the doors of the Oratorio were kept closed but this afternoon they were wide open to allow an effigy of the Crucified Christ to be taken out from it into the piazza on a wooden float carried by a band of porters, who supported the weight on their shoulders. Two other men also emerged from it bearing a funereal looking black and silver banner which was now giving trouble in the wind that was swirling around the piazza.

At the head of the procession was the rather elderly priest of Fosdinovo and Caniparola, dressed in black vestments. He was accompanied by a couple of acolytes, who were without their censers, because they were not used in such processions, and a good thing too, in the wind that was blowing, they might easily have set themselves on fire, or some other participant.

They were followed by the main body of the faithful, among whom we found ourselves. Altogether there were not many more than fifty people and most of them were women. There were also a few children; but it was not surprising that there was a poor turn-out. It was terrible weather for a procession. Already at around two in the afternoon it was growing dark.

Conspicuous among the few men present in the piazza, apart from those who would be carrying the images, looking benevolently at all and sundry, was Attilio who, we later learned, was not only *molto religioso* but also a *grande appassionato* of religious feasts and processions. He had walked up from I Castagni in the appalling weather in order to attend this one and, in spite of the buffering he must have received on the way, was very smart in a long, dark navy-blue, fur-collared overcoat of antique cut which almost reached to his ankles, and an article of clothing without which neither of us saw him, except when, later on, he had to go to hospital, his cap.

As soon as he saw us he came shooting across the piazza as if it was ice – in fact it was wet marble and equally slippery. Then, after paying his respects to the girls in a formal manner, he took our hands in his, first Wanda's, then mine, and pumped them up and down as if he expected water to come gushing out of our mouths, at the same time saying, so far as either of us could understand, how happy he was to see us.

But what was more extraordinary, so far as I was concerned, was that, when he began the pumping treatment he said, perfectly audibly, after having more or less cut me dead up to now, '*Adesso ricordo!*' ('Now I remember!')

What he said was mysterious, if not ambiguous. Unless I knew, which I now did without a shadow of doubt, that he, Attilio, and the old man in the mountains of twenty-odd years ago were not one and the same, I would have thought that when he said, '*Adesso ricordo!*' he was remembering that time, whereas what he was presumably referring to was our brief encounter five months ago. I gave up. Two storytellers, both of whom could make things, both of whom were *religioso*, one of whom, possibly both of whom, prayed by their bedsides, although there must be, I realized, whole hordes of little old men in Italy who do just that, were more than I could cope with. Eventually the whole thing was resolved when I asked Signora Angiolina if Attilio had ever gone away from home during the war. She said categorically no, he hadn't. I was sorry I asked. Perhaps it would have been better if it had remained a mystery but short of having a sphinx on the premises at I Castagni I could hardly complain.

Anyway I didn't care. What he had just said to me gave me the same feelings of pleasure that I would experience in the future when Signora Angiolina said to me *'Hai fatto bene!'* To be remembered by Attilio was different from being remembered by any Tom, Dick or Harry, or even General de Gaulle. He never enlarged on what he meant again. Now, however, to show where his sympathies lay, he attached himself, as it were, to our suite and prepared to walk with us in the procession.

It was at this moment that the priest gave some kind of inconspicuous signal, but one that was sufficient to set the whole thing in motion, and we all began to move uphill with the priest in the van, flanked by the acolytes, followed by Christ nailed to the Cross and the two men carrying the black and silver banner flapping madly in the wind, and behind them the main body of whom I was certainly the only Protestant present, snuffling and sneezing, for a number of them had already contracted nasty colds, sometimes chanting, sometimes reciting the rosary or saying various Lenten prayers, but somehow contriving not to do all these at the same time, which would have resulted in pandemonium.

The priest, although he looked rather old, was fearfully fit. He led us at what amounted to a trot into the teeth of the freezing wind and zoomed us through the winding streets and alleys, flanked by secretive-looking houses that made up Fosdinovo, mediaeval streets and alleys in which, this Friday afternoon, almost every house had at least one window with a candle burning in it, to welcome the procession.

Some windows were draped in funereal Lenten black, others were less lugubrious with white lace curtains and some were positively jolly with flowers displayed in them. We passed an ancient Malaspina theatre that was no longer a theatre and a Malaspina Mint that was no longer a mint. It only minted fifty genuine coins in its entire history. The rest, which were exported to Genova and France, were all false.

And there were shops, some of them minute, also illuminated with candles. Shops that sold wine, spades, handsaws and other ironware, hand-knitted socks with the natural grease still in them, and magazines giving the latest low-down on what was currently going on with the Grimaldis in the Principality of Monaco, events on which all Italy was hooked.

And we passed a *caffè* from the windows of which some of the male occupants looked out on the procession with the curious, slightly derisory air with which men in Italy look out of the windows of *caffès* at religious processions. That is if they are agnostic, communist, or simply not taking part in the procession for their own private reasons, keeping, as it were, their cards close to their chests.

That is also if they hadn't got wives or mothers or grandmothers taking part in these procession. If they had, and if they had any sense and wanted a quiet life, they would keep a much lower profile and get on with watching TV, or playing *briscola*, a sort of whist, and not start looking out of the window with that superior expression on their faces.

By now the wind was tremendous. At one point we came out on some ramparts below the Castello and there a savage blast caught the crucifix, bringing the bearers to their knees and almost throwing it to the ground, which would have been a *malaugurio* – and forcing the men carrying the banner to furl it.

Now we were rounding the foot of the keep of the Castello, a huge fortress in which Dante had been put up in 1306, while he wrote some stanzas of the *Inferno*, as he had apparently been, that same year, in the castle at Castelnuovo di Magra, the one we had seen the first time we had driven up the road from Caniparola, before making one of his mysterious disappearances from circulation. And as we were following this trench-like alley which ran between the dwellings and the walls, we could see the castle domestics looking down on us from overhead.

From now on most of the processional route was downhill. The first and last stop was at the Church of San Remigio in the middle of the town, the principal church of Fosdinovo.

Here the Crucified Christ was taken in, together with the now unfurled banner and followed by the rest of us, for the Adoration of the Cross.

Now the priest sang *Ecce Lignum Crucis* (Behold the Wood of the Cross), removed his shoes and adored it, prostrating himself three times and finally bending down and kissing the feet on the crucifix. Immediately after this the rest of the congregation went up to the crucifix two by two and prostrated themselves, while a number of *Improperia*, tender reproaches of Christ to his people, were sung, such as *Popule meus, quid feci tibi? aut in quo contristavi te? Respondi mihi.* (My people, what have I done to thee? or in what have I grieved thee? Answer me.)

The interior of the church was painted in a cold, bluish-grey colour, as cold as the air inside the church, and our breath smoked. Originally a Romanesque church, it had been destroyed by fire in 1600 and rebuilt as a baroque church by the Marchese Pasquale Malaspina with large numbers of magnificent side chapels, ornamented with alternating smooth and twisted Corinthian columns. It also had a barrel roof decorated with an abundance of frescoes but these were all destroyed in the fighting for the Gothic Line in the last year of the war when the town was bombarded.

In it under a Gothic arch, high up to the left of the altar, near the presbytery, was the tomb of Galeotto Malaspina, feudal lord of the region – the Malaspina acquired the castle in 1340 – and he died in 1367. Wearing armour his effigy reclined on a marble tomb chest, its panels ornamented with bas-reliefs.

Much higher still above the altar there was another marble effigy, carved by an unknown sculptor in the fourteenth century, the seated figure of San Remigio, patron saint of Fosdinovo, otherwise St Remigius, Bishop of Reims. Said to be the greatest orator of his age, on Christmas Day AD 496, he baptized Clovis, King of the Franks in the cathedral there, with the greatest imaginable pomp and ceremony, and the words, 'Bow thy head meekly, O Sicambrian. Adore what thou hast burnt and burn what thou hast adored.' (The Sicambrian cohort of the Franks was raised by the Romans on the spot where Budapest now stands.) Some of the bones of the saint were kept in the church at Fosdinovo in a silver reliquary ornamented with branching candlesticks.

For us this was the end of the procession. Now Christ was dead. We were all wet and cold but when I turned to offer Attilio a lift down the hill to I Castagni, he was nowhere to be seen and although I drove down several bends looking for him I failed to find him. He had simply melted away.

Chapter Seven

THE FOLLOWING morning, Holy Saturday, the world had a more cheerful aspect – cold, clear and almost cloudless, everything wet and sparkling after the rain.

There were even a few bold, migrant birds, some of which had the temerity to sing, making what would be, if they had any sense, only a brief touchdown in Italy before setting off for countries in higher latitudes whose inhabitants were more friendly to wild birds than the Italians who could only visualize them impaled on skewers and cooked.

Good Friday had been winter, with foul weather, black vestments for the clergy and altars stripped of everything, including the Host.

By comparison Holy Saturday was spring. Even Lent had lost much of its severity, with the clergy in violet and white vestments, white linen cloths spread on the altars in the churches, and grains of fresh incense set fire to by the priests with a flint outside the main door of the church, a fire that would subsequently be used to light the candles inside the building that had previously been extinguished.

We ourselves got up at six o'clock to start mobilizing helpers in the work of reconstructing I Castagni.

We got the keys of the house from Signora Angiolina who was already up long since, happy now that she knew that we were going to be, as she put it, *sempre con noi*, always with us, using the regal 'we', although we had made it clear that the most we could hope for would be a visit two or three times a year, and possibly a flying one while on the way to somewhere else. That is, unless I got the sack, in which case we would probably have to stay for ever.

We were really quite glad that she didn't offer to come down to the house with us but she did give us some eggs, some green salad, a bottle of wine and a loaf of delicious, newly baked bread.

But before all this we asked what news there was of Attilio, now playing one of his innumerable roles, this one his disappearing-into-thin-air-Attilio-the-Houdini-of-1 Castagni act. She said she hadn't seen him since the previous day, just after midday, when he had set off to take part in the procession, which was why she had had no idea that we had arrived in Fosdinovo. 'You did well,' she said, using her immortal phrase, 'not to have attempted to spend the night in the house in such weather. It might have ended badly.'

'Today,' she said, 'Attilio has gone to do *giornata*, and he may not be back here now for some days as the farm where he has gone to work is some distance beyond Fosdinovo, at a place called Foce il Cuccù [the Cuckoo's Mouth], but of course he won't work on Easter Day.'

Giornata meant that he had gone to work for someone and was being paid on a daily basis, either digging or hoeing or doing some other sort of farm work, or else repairing various agricultural instruments, making new handles for those which were broken, sharpening scythes and doing any other jobs Attilio was capable of performing. These, as we already knew, could be almost anything at all, providing that they weren't connected with engines, and he would probably even be able to deal with these, if the need arose.

'Attilio is one of those few people who will do a *giornata* any more,' Signora Angiolina said, 'because the pay is so bad. He should be paid much more. People take advantage of him.'

The most important item of news, however, that Signora Angiolina had to impart was that although Attilio was still sleeping in his little bedroom, and could continue to do so, so far as we were concerned, he had moved out of the kitchen. A neighbouring farmer had offered him the use of the kitchen which had its own water supply on the ground floor of one of his barns, while we were in residence at I Castagni.

'You know what he calls you now, Attilio?' Signora Angiolina said to Wanda as we got into the Land Rover to go down to the house in it for the first time, '*la mia padrona*', my boss.

The descent to I Castagni round the bend below Signora Angiolina's house turned out to be fraught with difficulty, even with a short-wheelbase Land Rover. It was a very tight and narrow bend with a tree on its inside edge which stood in relation to the bend itself as the central support does in a spiral staircase, while the outside edge of the bend overhung a steep bank about twenty feet high. At the foot of it there was a *vasca*, a common object in rural Italy, a large rectangular basin lined with cement, used for rinsing clothes, with an inclined marble slab at one end to squeeze and wallop them on. Its water supply came from a spring and was brought to it by a pipe in the bank which had a cork in it to conserve the supply. Whether it belonged to Signora Angiolina or someone else was not clear; but at this time, so far as we were concerned, nothing connected with I Castagni was clear.

On this first descent to the house in the Land Rover, trying to keep as close as possible to the inside of the bend, I contrived to get the rear hubcap hooked on to a stump on the side of the tree which made it impossible for me to go either backwards or forwards, or to open the door on the driver's side sufficiently for me to get out. A ludicrous mishap, of a sort I am peculiarly prone to, but not so ludicrous as the one that befell me the time I was driving from Milan to Venice in a jeep in thick fog and the accelerator pedal fell off.

'What has happened?' Wanda demanded in her best Slavonic imitation of the Marx Brothers' Margaret Dumont, one that for me always spells trouble.

'We're hooked on a tree,' I said. 'I'm afraid you'll have to get out, otherwise I can't get out either.'

She got out, rather reluctantly, I thought, as if she was doing me a favour.

'What I need is a saw,' I said, after a closer inspection of what had happened.

'You can't cut it down, it may not be ours.'

'I don't want to cut it down,' I said. 'I just want to cut a small bit off it.'

'Well, ask Signora Angiolina for a saw.'

'I don't want to ask Signora Angiolina for a saw,' I said. 'If it's anyone else's tree it's probably hers. It would be the worst possible thing to do, tell her I want to cut a bit off one of her trees, especially when we're getting on so well. You know what *contadini* can be like. Anyway we've got a saw of our own.'

'Where is it?' she said.

'I put it behind the front seat, the one you've been sitting on. You remember you told me not to bring it so I hid it.'

'I never told you not to bring it.'

'Well, that's what I thought you told me.'

'The trouble with you is,' Wanda said, 'you never listen.'

So I cut the offending protuberance off the tree with our saw and covered the scar with a bit of damp earth that was handy. Then, in what looked like unpropitious circumstances as far as our personal relationship was concerned, we drove on down to claim our property across the torrent, by which time the old I Castagni magic had re-asserted itself and we had become friends again. It had been a close thing as to whether we had a row – what Wanda calls a 'rowl' – or not and I promised myself that I would make it a priority to reinforce this crumbling outside curve by driving stakes into it with a sledge hammer and ramming in some hard core.

'Remind me to buy a sledge hammer and a crowbar when we go shopping,' I said to Wanda.

But of course she didn't and I never did reinforce the curve even though, although I didn't know it, there were already a number of hammers, some of them sledge, and a selection of crowbars on the premises. More urgent matters were to claim our attention, anyway, without bothering about a lump of stump the size of a matchbox.

When we arrived at the house a large frog was sunning itself on the wet grass in front of it, completely unafraid. It seemed to us at the time a good omen for the future.

When we finally managed to get the door of the kitchen open with the twisted key, the door which opened itself whenever there was a south-westerly wind of force 6 or above, we found that Attilio had done a great deal of work in the kitchen in anticipation of our arrival.

He had demolished the wattle-and-daub partition which had been infested with woodworm and carried it out behind the house and burned it. From now on, whenever we were at I Castagni, a fire burned almost all the time to dispose of the vast quantities of more or less inflammable material that had to be got rid of.

He had then swept the whole room clean, and the bedroom on the upper floor, and had sawn up an old, dead, iron-hard olive tree into logs of a manageable size for firewood with a primitive saw in which the tension of the blade was maintained by a twisted cord, and a double-bitted axe, a dangerous weapon with which one edge can be used for cutting, the other, more bevelled, for splitting – providing the user doesn't embed the top blade in his skull when raising it into the air. And he had collected a lot of dead chestnut branches and cut them up too, as well as providing a couple of bales of dried vine shoots which he had pruned after the previous *vendemmia*, the grape harvest, and which would make excellent kindling. There was even a sack of charcoal for the *fornello a carbone*.

Not only all this but somehow, using a couple of ladders, with what must have been, for one so small, a superhuman effort, he had managed to haul a huge old green tarpaulin over the most ruined part of the roof of the loft and secure it with ropes at the four corners.

But what expressed Attilio's sensibility more than anything else was that he had taken a saw to the wooden seat of the lavatory and had enlarged it to a size more suited to our adult proportions. What was clear was that Attilio would have to come on the payroll without delay.

'It's a bit difficult to know where to begin with the house,' I said. 'We need help, a lot of help.'

'The best thing we can do,' Wanda said, 'is to have something to eat and some of Signora Angiolina's wine. Then we'll go and look for a bricklayer and try and get a roof on the place.'

It was still only seven o'clock in the morning but we were terribly short of time. The next ten days were all we had at our disposal before we returned to England. In a moment of fantasy I wondered what would happen if I cabled the Editor of the *Observer*, and asked him if I was being missed, and if not, could I stay on for a bit longer; but I didn't wonder for long.

What we were in urgent need of were drains, a septic tank for them to gurgle their way into, and an inside lavatory. And where was the waste water from the mini-sink in the kitchen going at the moment? These were the sort of problems with which we were currently tormenting ourselves and which made it difficult for us to sit down and contemplate the rural scene.

In the loft we needed a completely new roof, apart from the tiles, the majority of which were sound but could fall and be shattered at any moment, but they didn't. It also needed a new floor or ceiling, according to whether we were upstairs or downstairs, with all the necessary beams and planking. We also had to have, as a matter of urgency, unless we were resigned to him dying of rheumatic fever, or some such similar complaint, a new roof for Attilio's room.

To do all these things we urgently needed the services of a plumber, a carpenter, and a *muratore*, a man who was both a bricklayer and a stonemason, each of whom would have to be fit enough to crawl all over this mouldering, highly dangerous structure without falling off it.

We were also going to need quite soon, if we were not to be electrocuted on the present amazing system in which an electric light bulb was soldered to the main, the presence of an electrician.

The upper part of the loft was going to be a bedroom with

access to it from the outside door at the back, the one in mid-air to which the only access at the moment was by a rickety ladder. The lower part was going to be a combined bathroom, lavatory, dressing room and storeroom.

It was the need to have the lavatory on the ground floor below what was going to be the bedroom in the loft that meant that it was going to be impossible to leave the ladder and the trapdoor where they were at present, giving access to the loft from inside the building. In future anyone residing in the loft wanting to use the bathroom would have to descend a ladder at the rear of the building and make a journey round two sides of it in the open air.

Perhaps we should have thought of this before we bought the house, but we didn't. What we now had to do was to render the floor/ceiling between the bathroom and the upper bedroom sound and smell proof. Eventually we were successful with the smells, with the sounds less so.

Now, in readiness for our first night on the premises, we blew up our airbeds and unrolled our sleeping bags, as we had done in many an uncomfortable spot throughout the world – the worst being a rat-infested railwaymen's institute on the banks of the Ganges. Remembering this Wanda elected to sleep on top of an old chest in case there were any mice in residence, the mice in these parts, according to Signora Angiolina, attaining the size of small cats.

We also tested the crazy electric light system which Signora Angiolina had told us how to switch on at the main and which, to our surprise, worked, but only in the kitchen.

After this we set off to drive a few bends up the hill to where the carpenter lived.

Chapter Eight

THE NAME OF THE carpenter was Alberto – he insisted on being called Alberto rather than its diminutive Berto, the Italian equivalent of Bert.

Alberto was just the sort of man we needed. He was young and agile and promised to come and look at the house the following Monday morning – Easter Monday. We asked him if he knew of a plumber, and he said he did, an older man called Bergamaschi, but a good one and he could ask him to come too.

Then we set off in search of the *muratore*, whose name was Renato. He lived in a nearby valley that terminated under the precipices on the east side of Fosdinovo.

Renato was a small man in his thirties with very bright blue eyes, as brown as a nut from a lifetime spent mostly in the open air, and full of energy. Things looked like getting off to a bad start at our first meeting when Wanda asked him if he was a *manovale*. In Italy a *manovale* means an unskilled labourer, the sort of labourer I was destined to be from now on, whereas Renato was a *muratore*, and a highly skilled one. For a moment it looked as if the meeting might come to an end there and then, but fortunately he had a sense of humour.

'I am a *muratore*, not a *manovale*,' he said, his eyes twinkling, 'but I have also been in my time a *manovale*.'

Renato lived in a smallish house in the middle of a fine vine-yard with his wife and three children, two small boys of about nine and eleven and a pretty daughter who was a couple of years younger. He was an ardent *cacciatore*. He owned several shotguns and rifles, there were piles of shooting magazines everywhere and the walls of his house were hung with trophies of the chase.

Renato constantly bemoaned the fact that to all intents and purposes *la caccia* in Italy was finished. He was now planning, together with a number of like-minded others, to release a couple of pairs of male and female wild boars, in a dense forest near the Foce il Cuccù, the pass to which Attilio had gone to do a *giornata*, in the hope that they would breed in sufficient numbers to make it worthwhile hunting them. There was no danger of the boar failing to procreate. They did so to such an extent that the area became infested with them.

In addition, hedging his bet as it were, he was saving up to go on a shooting holiday in one of the Iron Curtain countries, such as Yugoslavia or Bulgaria which, at that time, were arranging hunting expeditions for those who wanted to engage in such capitalistic activities as shooting bears, wild boar, deer, game birds, wolves and hares in exchange for large sums in foreign currency. In some of these countries the shoot had to be paid for in gold.

Besides being a good shot Renato also knew how to make really good wine in spite of this being, as we were beginning to find out after some sampling in depth, not a particularly good area for wine. The end product at that time had no denomination such as DOCG (*Denominazione de Origine Controllata e Garantita*) or DOC (*Denominazione de Origine Controllata*), or even DS (*Denominazione Semplice*), the humblest of all. When we began bottling our own wine, our son designed a label with a pen and ink drawing of the house and the words *Produzione Propria* on it.

Now Renato opened a bottle of his own red wine, something he was going to continue to do for all the years we were to know him, which made up for the somewhat meagre ration Wanda had imposed on us because it was still Lent. He, too, promised to come to the house on the morning of Easter Monday, but before we left he gave us what proved to be some useful advice.

'You won't have any difficulty in getting people like Alberto or Bergamaschi, to work for you, or even me, a *muratore*, a one-time unskilled labourer,' he said mischievously. 'But if you want us to continue to work for you we must be paid when we tell you we need the money. One of the curses of Italy is that if you are engaged in manual labour, whether skilled or unskilled, you can never get any money owing to you without a struggle. If you do eventually succeed it can take months, even years. So if you pay on time then you will have no trouble, word will soon get around and you will never lack for help.'

We followed his advice, only having work done that we could pay for at the time, and as a result no one who worked for us ever failed to do what we asked them to do – well almost none of them. In fact many years were to pass before things really changed for the worse, by which time what had previously been accomplished at I Castagni in a matter of months was no longer possible.

Our next stop was at the ironmonger's shop at Ponte Isolone. There we put in a crash order for things to be delivered that evening before dark: for a gas stove and a gas cylinder, a couple of rubber buckets of a sort that Renato assured us were indispensable to a *muratore*, a 'real' galvanized bucket, an assortment of brushes and brooms and one of those things you sweep all the dust into and then knock over, some sacks of cement, sand and a hosepipe with a connection that I hoped would fit the tap in the kitchen.

We were the first foreigners who had ever entered his establishment, the proprietor told us in a most uncharacteristic burst of confidence. Uncharacteristic because it was the last occasion, apart from greeting us formally at such ceremonies as weddings and funerals – '*Come sta, Signora, Signore?*' – that he ever addressed a single word to either one of us for a period of twenty-five years, apart from telling us the price of something in his shop or, when he rang up the till, how much we owed him.

After this we went back to the house to await the delivery – at least we were getting it free.

The goods arrived in a largish but rather feeble-looking van that was certainly not equipped with four-wheel drive, which the driver brought down round the bend and across the torrent with consummate ease, making me feel pretty silly. He then set up the gas stove, which was only a two-ring affair without an oven, on top of the *fornello a carbone* which Wanda understandably funked using.

The last act performed by the van driver before taking off up the hill and round the bend without touching the tree was to pour a Sahara of sand on to the ground outside what was going to be the bathroom before we could stop him, making it impossible for us to enter it, until I shifted it round to the back with a wheelbarrow, which took ages.

Chapter Nine

THAT EVENING OF Easter Saturday we found ourselves without any milk, having forgotten to buy any in Fosdinovo, and
by the time we got to the shop downhill from I Castagni it was
already shut.

'Rina will let you have some milk,' Signora Angiolina said.
'That's who I get it from, Rina Dadà. She'll let you have some for
sure. She is the wife of Tranquillo, the eldest son, and they have
a cow. She goes twice a day to the cowshed, at five in the morning and in the evening, to milk the cow.

'You should go and meet the family, anyway. They are all very
interested to know what you are like. And at the same time you
can make an agreement with Tranquillo about paying your share
of the water from La Contessa, the spring, because he is in charge
of it.

'They are a good family, the Dadà,' she went on. 'And
although they are *contadini* they are a sort of *famiglia reale* –
royal family – hereabouts and are very much respected.

'Take this bottle to put the milk in,' she said, 'and go now
before it's all gone. The cowshed is at the back, at the far end of
the house. Don't go round the front unless one of the family is
there because they have a dog on a chain, and it's a long chain.'

'Shouldn't you have a dog, Signora?' Wanda asked her. 'It's a
rather lonely place, isn't it, for a woman to be alone in?'

'I've got my cat,' she said. 'She's enough to be getting on with.
Besides, nothing bad ever happened to me, except once.'

'Why, what happened then?' Wanda asked.

'I'll tell you one day,' Signora Angiolina said.

The Dadà farmhouse was set back from the road and reached by a track at an acute angle to the main road, which was why we hadn't noticed it before.

The house was a solidly built, rather austere building, painted in *sangue di bue*, with only one of its windows visible from the side from which we were now approaching it, and it had a big chimney stack with smoke coming from it. Outside in the yard there were ploughs and harrows, a tractor and a big trailer with rear-wheel drive and mounds of logs cut for firewood, all now barely visible in the dusk.

Happy to be out of sight of what proved to be a thoroughly unpleasant dog we approached the shed from which deep bovine noises were emanating, and knocked on the door, at the same time saying, '*Permesso*?' and heard a female voice telling us to enter.

Inside it was very warm and it made me remember all the cowsheds I had slept in during the war, while on the run, and how happy I had always been whenever I was told that I could do so. You might suffocate in one but at least you were in no danger of dying of cold.

Illumination was supplied, as it always had been all those years previously, by an oil lantern and Signora Rina was sitting on a stool with her head alongside the cow's flanks, milking the beast. And, as it always had, the lamp cast fantastic shadows of the protagonists on the walls, distortions that used to remind me of Plato's 'Myth of the Cave'.

Signora Rina proved to be a slim, brown-eyed, brown-haired, very good-looking young woman, with finely delineated features, a Diana of the Hunt and the Moon, but one dressed in the *contadini* uniform: head scarf, cardigan, knee-length skirt, apron, thick, hand-knitted socks and clogs with leather uppers and wooden soles.

'Excuse me!' she said, 'I'm just finishing. Urrgh, *stai brava Bionda, brutta bestia!*' This to the cow who was doing her best to upset the results of their joint labours.

Seeing and hearing this I was back in the cowshed of Signor Ugolotti at Lagrimone in the Apennines of Parma, in the autumn of 1943. Then it had been a dark, wet night and I had asked him if I could sleep in his cowshed, or loft, while he was still milking – his cow was called Bella – and he had said no, I couldn't but I could have a bed, and I did, one that I have never forgotten.

And now, just as Signor Ugolotti, now dead, had done all those years ago, Signora Rina invited us into the house, into the room with the single window looking down the track towards the main road, which was the kitchen, past the now growling guard dog whose name was Mosso, which meant 'rough' in the sense of a rough sea, or simply 'troubled'. Mosso was both of these. There was no one else in the kitchen but something was cooking over a stove.

Then, when Signora Rina had poured the milk into the bottle Signora Angiolina had given us and we had paid her and had put in a similar order, night and morning, for as long as we were at I Castagni, she asked us if we would like to come to Easter Sunday lunch the following day. 'Then you will be able to meet some of our family,' she said.

In all the years we were to know Rina, and we still know her, neither of us ever saw her simply sitting down. If she was sitting then she was mixing or mending something. Otherwise she was always on her feet either in the fields, in the kitchen, or washing clothes, ironing or making *salsa di pomodoro*, or *pesto*, the green sauce of Genoese/Ligurian origin made with basil, garlic, *pecorino*, a hard cheese made from ewe's milk, soft when newly made, crushed pine nuts and olive oil, or cooking meals, or getting her son off to school, and so on. At that time, when we first met her, she was expecting what proved to be her second son.

Back at the house, having eaten supper in front of the fire, we retired to our sleeping bags on the upper floor. There Wanda balanced her airbed on top of the mediaeval chest; but it turned out to be impossible to sleep on as it had a domed lid. After falling off it twice she abandoned her attempt to spend a mouse-free night and joined me on the floor.

In fact there were no mice on duty either this evening or on any succeeding one as, according to their way of looking at things, spring had already broken out and they had left for the fields and would not be back until the autumn when we would really be able to appreciate the damage they were capable of wreaking on our clothing and bedding, all of which, including the mattresses, had to be wrapped up in thick plastic sheeting and suspended in mid-air from the ceiling on wires.

Sometime during the night, I became conscious of Wanda blundering about the room in the dark – I had dropped and broken the torch the previous evening – trying to find the exit to the staircase and the ground floor. What she wanted was a drink of water from the kitchen.

The next thing I heard was a cry of alarm, 'Eric! Help! *Aiuto! Aiuto! Ci sono dei scarafaggi!* There are thousands of *scarafaggi.*' Not having any idea what *scarafaggi* might be, I writhed my way out of my sleeping bag, groped my way to the stairhead where, still partly asleep, I tripped over a brick which was used as a doorstop and nearly did a swallow dive down the entire length of the stairs to the ground floor.

The light was on in the kitchen where an awful sight confronted me. Wanda was standing on Attilio's mini-chair looking down on what would have been the floor around the fireplace if it had not been almost entirely covered by a heaving brown sea of cockroaches, which were pouring in and out of a number of holes in the brick surround of the fireplace beneath which they presumably spent the hours of daylight.

If I had been a man of the calibre of my father I would probably have laid into them with a frying pan, something he had done years ago during a picnic on the River Thames to a swarm of wasps, having smeared the underside of the pan with jam, with disastrous results; but I knew when I was beaten. There was nothing to be done at this time of night, unless we could lay our hands on a blow lamp. What we really needed was a full-size *Flammenwerfer*.

I took Wanda on my shoulders, felt the cockroaches crunching under my bare feet and carried her crunch by crunch out of this now nightmare kitchen.

'You've forgotten to turn the light out!' Wanda said when I finally deposited her on cockroach-free ground at the foot of the staircase. She hates wasting electricity.

'Bugger the light!' I said – in the same tone of voice I imagine George V employed when told by his physicians that they were going to send him back to Bognor, 'Bugger Bognor!' – 'I'm not going back in there tonight. And how do you think I'm going to wash my feet, when the only water is either in the kitchen, or else somewhere outside down a well, for which we have a brand new galvanized bucket but no rope?'

'The trouble with you is,' Wanda said, 'you're always making difficulties. There's lots of wet grass.'

So I sat on the bottom step but one of the staircase and cleaned my feet with wet grass; but nothing would make me go back into the kitchen to put the light out.

✛

It was already daylight the following morning when I went down to the kitchen to find out the situation *vis-à-vis scarafaggi*, but apart from those I had squashed underfoot there were none to be seen. However there was very little comfort to be gained from this. They would certainly be back in force this coming night.

In theory nothing could be done until Easter Monday when those we called the *esperti*, the skilled men, were due to appear on the scene; but neither of us could face another irruption of this kind. What Attilio's attitude was to the *scarafaggi* was unclear. Perhaps he had always gone to bed before they surfaced and began their nocturnal revels. Perhaps they only emerged in the small hours of the morning. Whatever the answer we had to do something now.

'I'm going to get Renato,' I said to Wanda who was displaying the symptoms of someone who had been put on the rack, after spending a night on the floor on what proved to be a punctured airbed.

'You can't,' she said. 'It's Easter Sunday,'

'I don't care if it's Guy Fawkes Day,' I said. 'It's only seven o'clock in the morning. Someone's got to help us.'

So I went to see Renato.

He asked me if I had a pick and I said there were several on the premises all belonging to Attilio. Then we set off, Renato having first of all armed himself with a blow lamp.

With the picks we dug up the brick floor of the fireplace and the surrounds and then Renato proceeded to burn out a seething mass of creatures from what must have been age-old nests. Even he was impressed by what we discovered, judging by the number of times he used what was his favourite expression, '*porca miseria*'.

The smell created by this fry-up was indescribable, but from that time onwards we never saw another cockroach there or anywhere else in the house. Presumably the fireplace had been the only part of it warm enough to attract them. Neither of us had any scruples about destroying them. Either the *scarafaggi* were going to continue to live at I Castagni, or we were. They had not formed part of the dreams I had dreamt while locked up in Germany.

This was the morning that Wanda began to plant numbers of roses, Queen Elizabeths, that she had brought from England. In a few years Queen Elizabeths would be proliferating all over the area grown from Wanda's cuttings.

Years later a swarm of hornets took up residence somewhere deep in the walls of Attilio's 'secret' room, from which they emerged to drone around our heads but without ever actually attacking us. Nevertheless, it was an unnerving experience and, advised by one of our neighbours, I decided to smoke them out.

I expected to be attacked while carrying out this operation but in fact the only thing the hornets were interested in doing was saving their young. I felt like a murderer.

Chapter Ten

WHAT HAD BEEN, until the arrival on the scene of the *esperti*, a little comedy as it were with a modest cast of half a dozen or so and about the same number of walk-on parts, would now be augmented by the emergence on stage of more and more supporting talent, much of it up to now hidden away from view in the all-embracing undergrowth, or else out of sight within the walls of buildings to which we had not yet gained admittance, or had not yet even seen.

Sometimes, if there was a *festa*, or a sale of cattle, or a funeral, or a wedding, or a meal given to those who were participating in a *vendemmia*, then the cast, swollen temporarily by the enrolment of extras, could amount to hundreds so that at times I used to wonder if we were participating in a Cecil B. de Mille epic or something like a musical without the music.

At around half-past twelve on Easter Sunday, having swept away the last of the now all dead *scarafaggi*, and having had a very perfunctory wash in a basin that was the size of the smallest sort of holy water stoup, we put on what were the best clothes we had available and presented ourselves at the kitchen door of the Dadà farmhouse, Mosso the dog having been locked up for the occasion.

In view of what Signora Angiolina had told us about the family we were not without a certain feeling of trepidation when we said, '*Permesso*?' and knocked on the door, but it turned out that our fears were groundless. We could not have been given a warmer welcome.

The only other time we had seen the kitchen had been by the light of Rina's oil lamp the previous evening. Now it could be seen to be much larger than it then appeared to be. At one end there was a big open fireplace with, to one side of it, a wood-burning cooking stove which you could sit around on cold days, and on the other a *fornello* of the sort that Wanda had just replaced with a gas ring. Both these cookers now had various pots and pans seething away on them.

Against another wall there was a *madia*, and an *armadio a muro*, both more or less twins of our own. The centre of the room was taken up by a rectangular table covered with a dazzlingly white cloth and laid for what looked like a major lunch. There was no television, and wouldn't be for some time to come; only a battered radio and that was switched off.

It was Rina who had been doing the cooking with Signora Maria, Rina's mother-in-law, giving a helping hand. She was a short, good-looking woman in her fifties, with her hair drawn back in a bun, and she emanated a tremendous air of authority, of a sort that she knew she would only rarely have to exercise – the Head of the Family, the *capo famiglia* personified. Signora Angiolina had been right about the *famiglia reale* with women such as Rina and Signora Maria on the distaff side.

Now, as in a play, or it could have been a coronation, other members of the family began to appear.

First Signor Modesto, Signora Maria's husband, the *capo famiglia*, and their eldest son, Tranquillo, Rina's husband. They both entered through another door bearing large bottles and straw-covered *fiaschi* of red and white wine that they had been drawing off from one or other of the many large, wicker-covered glass demijohns, which each held up to fifty-five litres of wine, in the neighbouring cellar. Here, as in many other farms in Italy, the wine cellar was at ground level, rather than underground.

Signor Modesto was about the same height as his wife and about the same age and apparently as diffident as his name implied; but in spite of his gentle aspect he was really a redoubtable character. Together they made a redoubtable pair.

Once we saw them digging a field together, each using a *vanga*, a long-handled spade with a triangular blade, shoulder to shoulder, plunging the blades into the earth and turning the clods in perfect unison, a remarkable sight and one that would soon cease to be seen at all, now that even these small, hillside fields were already beginning to be cultivated with the aid of tractors and machinery.

Tranquillo was taller than his parents, without an ounce of spare flesh on him and with a deeply lined face. At that time he must have been in his late twenties. He was a quiet man. When not working the family property he spent much of his time in the huge forests beyond Fosdinovo, cutting wood. It was his trailer, loaded with what would be firewood when it was cut into more manageable chunks, that was now standing in the yard outside.

Tranquillo also hired himself and his tractor and various sorts of agricultural machinery to other farmers.

And there was Tranquillo's younger brother, Valentino, a rather pale, quiet, intelligent boy who was still at school and wanted to be an engineer. If he succeeded in realizing this ambition he would be the first of the family to leave the land.

And there was Paolo, the son of Tranquillo and Rina.

There were no pre-lunch drinks as there would have been in Britain. Such *aperitivi* were unknown in rural Italy. No hanging about either. As soon as the quorum of participants at the feast had been made up someone uttered the magic words, '*Avanti, andiamo a tavola!*' and we went to the table.

The meal was predominantly Tuscan with some Ligurian additions. First of all we ate *bruschetta*, a dish that is Tuscan through and through – slices of homemade bread toasted over the open fire, a job that had fallen to Valentino, until they were brown on the outside and still soft inside; then rubbed on both sides with cloves of garlic that had been cut in two before having the new season's olive oil poured over the toast, oil made from olives that had been laboriously hand-picked the previous winter. These were gathered using special baskets, worm-eaten examples of which we had seen in Attilio's 'secret' room. By now it was becoming more common for farmers to suspend nets under the branches of the olive trees and then shake them down when the olives were ripe; but many people, including the Dadà, believed that the oil made from olives harvested in this way was inferior to that made from olives gathered by hand.

The olive harvest was no light matter. A family the size of the Dadà needed something like a hundred litres of oil or even more to see them through the year; and a *quintale* of olives, a hundred kilos, yielded between ten and twelve litres of oil, a figure that varied from year to year, sometimes more, sometimes less when it was pressed at the *frantoio*, the olive press, of which there were several in the neighbourhood.

With the *bruschetta* we began to drink the wine, the red or the white but not mixing them. Then came the *salami*: *prosciutto di Parma*, air-cured in barns in the foothills on the far side of the Apennines in the Province of Parma, the best ham of all being made from the pigs fattened on the hillsides above the Pianura Padana, the great plain of the Po, served here and now because, although not of local origin, it was better than any other.

And there was *mortadella* but not what was generally meant by *mortadella*, a large Bologna sausage that ought to be pure pork[*] cooked by a steam process and flavoured with coriander and white wine. Here in this part of Tuscany, it was a raw, salt-cured *salame* of irregular shape, good, but not as good as the *salame* of Felino, a village near Parma. Not as good as the *culatello di Zibello*, a village on the banks of the Po, part of the pig's bottom, the most expensive of all, a delicacy which Gabriel d'Annunzio, that eccentric and erotic patriot, once compared for sweetness in a cannibalistic moment to the breasts of a beautiful woman. Not as good, but good, this *mortadella* made in wintertime and eaten now with pickled gherkins and homemade bread, still warm from the oven.

---

[*] *Ought* to be but, according to Elizabeth David, *Italian Food* (1963), 'may be a mixture of pork, veal, tripe, pig's head, donkey meat, potato or soya flour and colouring essence'.

After the *mortadella* and the *bruschetta*, which was more fill-ing than it perhaps sounds, came *lasagne al forno*, squares of pasta made with eggs – first cooked in salted, boiling water before being transferred to a dish in which layers of it alternated with *ragù* and a thick *besciamella* sauce. They were then baked in an outside oven until they became a beautiful brown colour. This *ragù* was made with onion, celery, carrot, parsley, minced lean beef and chopped *pancetta*, part of the pig's stomach, a sort of bacon, and *conserva di pomodoro*, preserved tomatoes put into glass jars the previous summer when they were at their ripest and reddest. The *besciamella* was made with flour, milk and butter, salt, black pepper and either grated *pecorino*, or else *grana*, hard Parmesan cheese, which by this time was already extremely expensive.

Sometimes Rina varied the menu at this point by substituting *tortellini al sugo* for the *lasagne*, little packets of pasta filled with a stuffing of which there were innumerable variants, often made from lean pork and veal, breast of capon, ham, brains, *mortadella* (the Bolognese sort), *grana*, eggs, butter, salt, pepper and nutmeg, a considerable work.

So far as Wanda and I were concerned, by the time we had eaten our way through the *lasagne* and had failed to refuse a sec-ond helping, both of us had had more than enough; but it was now that the oven yielded up another masterpiece, *pollo arrosto*, a free-ranging chicken that had spent its life in the Dadà farmyard, now cooked in olive oil and with a tiny bit of butter to brown it, which Rina had basted with a sprig of rosemary and served with potatoes that had been roasting in the juices given off by the chicken; and with it there was served a very young, green salad.

After this there was a short interval while fresh, creamy *pecorino* was on offer but there were few takers.

It was now that one of Modesto's sweet table wines made its appearance to accompany the final major offering, *tiramisù*, liter-ally 'pull me up', a very fattening sweet made with *mascarpone*, an unsalted cream cheese made in winter with cow's milk and sold in Tuscany, and other parts such as Lombardy, in little muslin bags; the cheese mixed with sugar, egg yolks, cognac, rum or some sort of *liquore*.

Then walnuts and coffee, which could be *corretto*, spliced with something strong.

So far as I was concerned it was fortunate that, during this copious luncheon, not all that much conversation was directed at me personally. I lacked the capacity that most Italians possess of being able to carry on an animated conversation with their mouths full of *lasagne al forno*, or even more amazingly full-length spaghetti, without displaying the contents of their mouths to those facing them across the table or dropping them into their laps. If any one of the other participants had decided to engage me in an extended exchange of ideas I would have found myself at least one course behind the rest of the company. Wanda, who had spent most of her formative years in Italy, was more adept at keeping up.

Much of the talk was about the vines and the sowing of seeds. This was the time of year when much of the pruning of the vines took place, and it was now that the *contadini* sowed their vegetable seeds, everything from peas to parsley.

That is if the moon was a *luna calante*, waning, not a *luna crescente*, waxing. With a *luna crescente* no one in their right minds would begin to season a ham, or buy anything that could possibly wither or fall to pieces, even furniture. Meanwhile, Valentino, Tranquillo's younger brother, asked me the same questions I had had to answer during the war about the prevalence of pea-soup fogs in London, something that all *contadini* still believed, and still believe, to be endemic there. He had been disappointed when I told him that the last one of any consequence had been in December 1952 and had lasted four or five days, but cheered up when I said it was a very thick one.

And over the *caffè corretto*, Tranquillo told me about an enormous Italian gun secreted in a concrete casemate on the island of Palmaria across the Gulf of Spezia from Lerici. Manned by the Germans or Fascist Italians in 1945, in the last stages of the war here, on the extreme right of the Gothic Line, it had bombarded the area around Fosdinovo, scaring everyone stiff. Meanwhile the Allies had lobbed large numbers of shells into Fosdinovo. But it was the sheer size of the projectiles that came from Palmaria that had impressed Tranquillo.

'The first thing we saw when it was fired,' he said, 'was this great flame coming out of a cliff at the east end of the island. Then after that we used to count to four, I can't remember exactly how much, and we could hear the shell coming towards us, with a noise like an express train. And when it exploded it made a hole big enough to put a bus in. Luckily for us they only had enough ammunition for about twelve shots. Then they ran out. We were in a ditch all the time until they did. The only damage was a big crack in one of the walls of the house, and eventually the Alleati paid for the damage.'

It was almost five o'clock before the proceedings finally came to a halt and we were given a positively regal send-off by the entire family which had assembled in the yard. It had been a memorable occasion and although we did not know it at the time, we had been accepted.

✛

Later, the thing I most enjoyed doing when we were at I Castagni was going with Tranquillo into the great forests around Fosdinovo to load his trailer, with the wood he had cut with a chainsaw the previous year. (Using a cross-cut saw would have involved hiring an extra man, which was why no one used them any more.)

On these journeys we visited places into which it seemed impossible that anyone could take a tractor, let alone a trailer and return with it, loaded to the equivalent of the gunwales, in fact much higher than the gunwales because he set up stakes vertically around the edge of it that enabled it to be loaded to a far higher level than would otherwise have been possible; after which the whole load had to be lashed down with ropes.

I could only admire Tranquillo's consummate skill on the

return journeys to what seemed like the outside world when he hauled the trailer up through rocky gorges in which the air was full of the sounds of waterfalls, and skirted the edge of precipices on tracks that were often pot-holed and deep in mud. In these moments I began to feel that I was a 'real' *contadino*, something I could never be.

✠

Going down the hill, past Signora Angiolina's place – she had gone to spend the evening with her sister – we were engulfed in the peculiar kind of melancholy that envelops one after a prolonged luncheon when one finds oneself all of a sudden in the open air, bound for an unheated house. So that evening we went and had a modest meal in La Scaletta on the outskirts of Sarzana, which became our favourite restaurant. In it the food was *cucina casalinga*, the sort that Italian mothers turn out for all their working lives.

Later La Scaletta was the scene of a spectacular mishap when having celebrated a nice review of my latest book and having become 'over excited' in the process, I fell down the entire flight of steps from which the restaurant took its name, measuring my length in the road below and hurting myself considerably. Fortunately, Wanda was away at the time visiting her mother. And it was the proprietor, Signor Tito, who took me home.

The meeting with the skilled men, the *esperti*, at least we hoped they were, took place at an early hour on Easter Monday. Mercifully, it wasn't raining.

There was Alberto, the carpenter, Bergamaschi, the plumber, who was the oldest, about sixty-five, and there was Renato, the stonemason. He arrived on an old Lambretta with his small son on the pillion seat. There had been no point in summoning an electrician at this stage of the proceedings as there were such huge voids in the fabric of the building, the equivalent of black holes, that in many places there was literally nothing to which the wires could be attached.

Among those present, the only one with any kind of transport was Renato. Scarcely anyone up there in the hills at that time owned anything in the way of a motor vehicle. There were still some pack mules, but these were already becoming rare at such low altitudes. Cycling was out of the question, unless one was training for the Giro d'Italia, the equivalent of the Tour de France. This meant that if any of our *esperti* needed to bring any materials to the site they either had to hire a van, or else find someone with a tractor and a trailer, such as Tranquillo, and pay them. It was lucky that we had a Land Rover. In the following week we were able to move quite a lot of stuff but it was a pity it was only a short-wheelbase model, which meant that it had very little room in it.

Also on site was Attilio, who was to do as much as anyone to help us in this time of need. He had emerged from what was to us the still undiscovered country around the Foce il Cuccù, no doubt because some equivalent to a bush telegraph had informed him that something important was going on down the hill that merited his presence.

Now he stood on the eminence on which the sale of the property had been negotiated, accepting with equanimity the various affectionate pleasantries that were being bandied around by the *esperti*, such as 'Been doing any flying lately, Attilio?', things that would have been gibberish to us unless we had been briefed by Signora Angiolina, and at the same time discomfiting them by going into his 'Heh! Heh! Heh!' act, the one I liked the best.

From time to time he disappeared into the 'secret' room in search of various tools when any of the others asked for a loan of them. For, just like *esperti* everywhere in the world, they preferred to borrow other people's tools rather than wear out their own.

It would be tedious to attempt to describe everything that was agreed and arranged between ourselves and the *esperti* that Easter Monday.

With Attilio's ladders leaning against the walls and Renato and Alberto up on the roof, with parts of it already removed in order that some exploratory work could proceed, the scene brought to mind an Irish eviction during the Hungry Forties in some such place as Skibbereen, with Attilio on his little hill, playing the part of the aged, evicted tenant to perfection.

Meanwhile Signor Bergamaschi, whose face was so pock-marked that it resembled a close-up of part of the surface of the moon, had turned his attention to the plumbing.

What he was really interested in discovering was the where-abouts of the septic tank, that is if there ever had been one. Attilio was not a mine of information on the subject of plumbing.

Eventually after prodding around on one of the terraces below the house, using a sort of dipstick, Signor Bergamaschi found the tank when it sank up to the hilt in what appeared to be solid earth. It proved to be a tank in such a spectacularly awful state, having failed to perform its biodegradable functions for a long time, that he decided that I should dig another, larger one and that when I had done this, Renato should line it with bricks and mortar, also with my assistance. '*E un merdaia*' (a shit heap) was how Signor Bergamaschi described it, and he could scarcely be accused of exaggerating.

When I had done all this, Signor Bergamaschi said, dangling a carrot before me that I found difficulty in resisting, we should be able to have a water heater, a wash basin, a shower, a lavatory basin and even, unimaginable luxury, a bidet, all this in what was still a stable, and we could also have a bigger sink in the kitchen, instead of something that resembled a holy water stoup. But of all these it was the thought of the bidet that really hooked me. At last something in which to wash my rubber boots.

To realize this dream, and damn near kill myself in its execu-tion, in the next couple of days I dug a hole in one of the terraces below the house and some distance from the abandoned *merdaia*, in clay that looked like over-cooked steak and was as difficult to work. It was twelve feet square and five feet deep and to do it I used a pick and one of Attilio's triangular-bladed spades.

From it I dug trenches up to the house which would carry the waste pipes from the kitchen and the soon-to-be-emergent bathroom, which I hoped would take care of our combined wastes for some time to come. And indeed, apart from an occasional hiccuping sound which the tank emitted when the house was overflowing with guests who insisted on pouring detergent into it and other inimical noxious substances, and an occasional wave of gaseous smells when the wind was in the south-west, it did take care of them.

No sooner had I finished digging the hole for the septic tank than I found myself promoted to being Renato's assistant, in the position of *manovale*, one which I shared with his youngest son who already knew more about the work of a *muratore* than ever I would.

From now on my more or less permanent task whenever I worked with Renato was mixing cement to whatever was the consistency he required; in this case first of all for the septic tank and then, when that was done, carrying buckets of it up to him on one or other of the roofs on one or other of the numerous ladders which had been set up against the walls, giving the impression that the house was a besieged city that had been taken by storm.

Once up there I was sometimes permitted a couple of minutes respite to admire the view and Renato's skill with a trowel, before being sent below once more with his urgent cry of '*Ancora un po' di cemento!*' ('More cement!') ringing in my ears.

Meanwhile the orders for various materials came pouring in, most of them placed by Signor Bergamaschi: plastic piping – we were lucky, a few years previously it would have had to be lead – a meter for the water supply, and a valve to reduce the pressure of La Contessa, the spring having such a head on it according to him that, uncontrolled, it could blow a hole in an electric water heater of the sort he was proposing to install in the bathroom. This, about the power of La Contessa, proved to be only too true when, having taken delivery of a rather tinny-looking water heater from a builders' merchant in Sarzana down the hill, he connected it up with the water supply without setting the valve to the correct pressure, with the result that the water, as he had foretold, blew a hole clean through it.

Most people would say that this was a misfortune that Signor Bergamaschi had brought upon himself but all he did was to take the heater back to the supplier, complaining that it was defective, whereupon they gave him a replacement free of charge. Tinny-looking it might be but this Velodoccia lasted us for twenty-five years and, for all I know, may still be functioning.

We also took delivery of a load of tiles and several large cans of Vellutina, a sort of whitewash.

The only material we seemed to have a superfluity of was sand. This was the sand that I had moved to the back of the house from the entrance to the bathroom in a series of what seemed innumerable wheelbarrow journeys because with it where it was we couldn't open the bathroom door. I also thought it was better out of sight. But Renato didn't. '*Non l'ha messo nel luogo giusto! Bisogna spostarla!*' ('You haven't put it in the right place! You must move it!') was the first thing Renato said when he saw where I had put it. So I did, carrying it round to the front of the house again in another series of what seemed endless wheelbarrow journeys, where the residue remained for twenty years in case he might need it.

At the same time there were what ought to have been comic interludes but weren't particularly when all four of us – Renato, Alberto, Bergamaschi and myself – were up in the loft, trying to rid it of the coils of wire which more or less filled it, wrestling with it, rather like the Laocoöns in their death agonies, beset by iron snakes.

That Monday morning, while Wanda was making coffee for the assembled company, an old man came steaming up the hill and halted outside our kitchen door.

He was about five feet five, had white hair, a white moustache, a good show of white stubble on his cheeks, a white shirt, a white tie, a black suit, a beautiful black felt Borsalino hat and black, well-polished mountain boots. It was difficult to know how old he was but he was very sprightly. His name was Anselmo and everyone knew him, including Attilio, who took his hand and shook it vigorously.

Apparently he had been a *mezzadro* and he lived in one of the Malaspina houses on what was a short cut down to Sarzana, but his real skill was in making the big wooden sleds with wattle sides until comparatively recently used to bring wood down from the forests. His wife didn't go out much as she had arthritis. He was now on his way to a house further up the hill where he went to be shaved every Monday morning. The reason why he was shaved on Monday when all barbers' shops in Italy are closed, was that this barber did it as a favour to Anselmo on what was his day off.

'I'm just making some coffee,' Wanda said to him, '*Vuol favorire?*', using the expression, 'Will you do us the favour of having some?'

'No, *grazie*,' Anselmo said. '*A me il caffè fa male.*'

'*Allora, un bicchierino di grappa?*' Wanda said, producing a big bottle of the stuff that had been distilled by one of her relatives in Slovenia, across the frontier near Trieste.

He didn't say 'no' so she poured him a two finger glass; and then, quite suddenly, it was gone. It was strong stuff. '*Vado a farmi la barba,*' Signor Anselmo said to no one in particular, having refused a second dose, 'Now I am going to be shaved,' put himself in bottom gear and zoomed over the torrent, up the hill, round the bend, and past Signora Angiolina's house for his appointment with the barber, as if he was propelled by rocket fuel, which was more or less what Wanda had given him.

For many, many years every Monday morning whenever we were in residence, Signor Anselmo used to drop in on his way to have a shave and, every so often, a haircut in a house up the hill that we never saw. He didn't really drop in. Like all the rest of our male visitors he always used to hum some song or other just sufficiently long before he actually arrived on the scene for Wanda to be ready with a bottle to furnish him with a *bicchierino*, a stirrup cup without a stirrup. He never actually entered the premises, even when it was raining as he had an umbrella.

He always went home by a different route, Signor Anselmo, presumably so as not to bother us further. He was a man of sensibility.

Then, one Monday, he failed to appear and never came again. He had died while we were in England. Everyone assumed that we would know that he had gone, and so no one told us, not even Attilio.

✠

According to Alberto, the carpenter, the problem was where was he going to be able to lay his hands on some well-seasoned timber for the floors, for joists and roof beams and for a complete set of windows and shutters. 'All I can get from the merchants is junk,' he said. 'I think the best chance is with one of the *demolizioni*,' he went on. 'They have a lot of seasoned wood. What I would like for the floors would be old deck planking; but it will be full of nails and it can be very expensive.'

'What are these *demolizioni*?' Wanda asked.

'*Demolizioni* buy up all the removable parts of ships when they go to the shipbreakers – the *demolitori di Navi*. Most of these *demolitori* have their yards near La Spezia at the head of the Gulf, just over the hill from here, beyond the Magra.' (La Spezia was one of Italy's principal naval bases.)

'Where can we find one of these *demolizioni*?' I asked him.

'There are a couple down beyond Sarzana where the road bridge crosses the Magra. If you like I will take you there. We could go this afternoon,' Alberto said, 'after the *merenda*.' The *merenda* is a snack, or a picnic. All the *esperti* had brought one with them, except Renato who went home for his midday meal, taking his son with him on his Lambretta.

'But it's Easter Monday,' Wanda said. 'Surely they won't be open?'

'*Demolizioni* usually only close when it's too dark to see your money. I wouldn't be surprised if they opened on Easter Sunday,' Alberto said.

Together the three of us drove down to the left bank of the Magra where a couple of the *demolizioni* were situated. It was an area of peculiar squalor, one that had until quite recently been almost arcadian, now the sort of place where people shot their rubbish and made themselves scarce.

Here, in the shadow of the bridge, under the abutments, now that the air was growing colder, a couple of tarts, probably despairing of drumming up any business on Easter Monday afternoon, had deserted their posts on the approaches to the bridge and were warming themselves over a fire made from discarded cardboard boxes.

So far as the *demolizioni* were concerned, there was very little to choose between them. Each was surrounded by corrugated iron fences with the tops cut into spikes. Both were guarded by Germanic-type dogs, four to each compound, which patrolled the perimeters on running wires.

Made free to go where we wanted, after the dogs had been called off, we drifted down avenues on either side of which an extraordinary variety of marine objects were thrown up, as if by some gigantic storm: Carley floats, life belts, rafts, sidelights, huge swathes of rope and chain, blocks, bo's'ns' chairs, teak pin-rails from sailing ships still equipped with belaying pins, binnacles, mahogany chart-houses, fire extinguishers, engine room telegraphs, companion ladders, lifeboats, bundles of oars, signs that read 'First Class Saloon' and 'To the Swimming Bath', teak gratings, fog horns, rockets, enormous white ventilators, anchors, hundreds of ash trays, cane chairs and wooden ones with extension pieces on the arms for first-class passengers to put their feet up on while drinking beef tea, signal flags, wash basins as big as fonts, mahogany-panelled lavatory basins with a vertical flushing handle which, when you pulled it, gave you the feeling that you were bombing a city, stacks of timber, including masts and planking.

Eventually we ended up buying a whole lot of pine planking that had come out of a ship built around 1903, and some beams to support them. The only wood we couldn't find was for the window frames and shutters, and it had to be bought new elsewhere.

The terms included free transport to I Castagni, cash on delivery. Alberto had exaggerated the toughness of the proprietor. The only snag was, as Alberto had predicted, that the planking was full of nails. He gave the job of extracting them to his young son, which he accomplished in two evenings, after school. He was paid the going rate for anyone pulling six-inch nails out of old ships' planking.

The visit to the *demolizioni* also yielded a number of other useful objects: a teak stepladder that would be useful for reaching the door in the back wall of the loft, the one up in the air, and a couple of teak gratings for the floor of the bathroom; but what I would really have liked was a fog horn. Never mind, I was getting a bidet, you can't have everything in this world.

The next week went like a flash; but it wasn't so bad because we knew that we could rely on the *esperti*. By a stroke of good fortune Renato was able to work a full day every day, instead of only a few hours in the afternoon and evening after his 'real' work was finished.

In the course of it he and Alberto, with a bit of help from me in my guise of carrier of raw materials up ladders, were able to put a new roof on Attilio's bedchamber, and on most of the loft.

During this time Bergamaschi managed to get the plumbing in all the way down the trenches I had dug as far as the septic tank; and when he was quite sure the pipes weren't going to leak all over the place, he told me to fill the trenches in. I filled them in.

Before doing this, early on Tuesday morning, Wanda and I made a flying visit to a couple of marble yards near Carrara in order to find a sink for the kitchen and a wash basin for the bathroom. There we were able to acquire, ready-made, a kitchen sink, a wash basin and a draining board, all fashioned out of gleaming white marble. And by that evening all these and the shower were in position.

With the plumbing in it was now possible to dig up the cobbles under the shower in the bathroom and for Renato to cement and tile that part of the floor where the waste pipe was. We left the rest of the cobbles where they were for the time being. Although picturesque they were impossible to keep clean, and eventually they had to be replaced by tiles, which would have cost a fortune if I had not been given a lot of old ones by Tranquillo. Unfortunately most of them still had rock-hard cement on their backs, which had to be chipped off with a hammer, which took me ages. That same year, Renato transformed the kitchen and the living room by flooring them with *terrazzo*, made by setting marble chips into a layer of mortar and polishing the surface.

It was this afternoon that Bergamaschi performed his famous *coup de main* with the water heater. That same afternoon we also got hold of an electrician, Signora Angiolina's nephew, her sister's son, to put in some temporary wiring. We could now have hot showers.

While all this was going on Wanda whitewashed the whole interior of the house, with the exception of Attilio's 'secret' room, giving it two coats of Vellutina, a huge job, but at least it looked more cheerful. The worm-eaten floor of the loft would have to be replaced while we were back in England, using the planking and the joists we had bought from the *demolizioni*. The big tree trunk that was the principal support of the roof in our upstairs bedroom – the one that was split almost from end to end – was fitted with a wrought-iron collar, made by Attilio, a miniature Vulcan at his forge, and never gave any more trouble. And finally we painted the floor of the fireplace in the kitchen, what we hoped was the permanent tomb of the *scarafaggi*, a deep, appropriately mournful shade of *sangue di bue*.

Each evening, too done-in to bother about cooking, we each had a delicious hot shower and then drove down to the Arco, the little *trattoria* at Caniparola, for supper.

The son of the Signora who ran the place was studying to be an architect at Pisa, but when he was at home he used to help out by acting as a waiter. It was he who later arranged to take us to see the splendid baroque interior of the Malaspina villa. The Signora's female assistant, who also did some of the cooking, was ginger-haired and rustic. What we were given there was simple home cooking, the sort described as *nostrano*.

✠

By the end of this punishing week, with only a couple of days to go before we were due to leave for England, we were both beginning to feel that there must be something a bit more entertaining than spending twelve hours a day making I Castagni habitable, which it certainly wasn't going to be this time round, or this coming autumn either, unless we found some beds.

So when Signora Angiolina suggested that we might like to go on a wild asparagus hunt, and take Attilio with us – apparently she had a bit of land about half a mile away on which wild asparagus grew – we were happy to accept her invitation. 'It's a good year for *asparagi selvatici*,' she said.

The following morning, armed with baskets to put the asparagus in – always a rash thing to do, take a basket in anticipation when looking for temperamental, unpredictable wild growths such as asparagus and *funghi* – we set off in Indian file for the asparagus field, with Signora Angiolina leading the way and Attilio bringing up the rear, talking away, if to anyone, probably to Wanda, '*la mia padrona*', occasionally coming to a halt in order to observe more closely some previously unnoticed wonder of the world which had presented itself for his delectation, rather as my father used to when confronted in the street by someone with a bottle nose.

We followed a series of grassy footpaths that passed beneath long pergolas of vines, from time to time skirting barns that gave the impression, quite wrongly, of being disused, and small houses, some of them a bit similar to I Castagni of which we and Attilio were the occupiers.

On one occasion early on in our occupation of I Castagni we visited one of these houses and took away some implements under the impression that it was an abandoned house, only to find to our horror that it wasn't.

The only sorts of asparagus I had eaten up to now were herbaceous varieties grown from seed which, after a slow beginning, emerged from the well-manured soil in which they had been planted, as vegetables of various lengths and diameters bearing some resemblance to miniature ballistic missiles, although other comparisons as to their appearance have been made.

What we were now, all four of us, confronted with in Signora Angiolina's field, which was much wilder than any English field, or any other field I had seen anywhere, for that matter, was something very different. Cultivated asparagus was taken from the earth. These *asparagi selvatici* were waving about in mid-air and thin enough to be very nearly invisible. It was now that I discovered that I had left my bifocals at I Castagni which, so far as gathering wild asparagus was concerned, rendered me more or less *hors de combat*. All I could see were the hands of the other three when they snatched the asparagus out of what should have been, if I had only had my glasses, my field of vision.

At the end of half an hour the entire crop had been harvested. Signora Angiolina and Attilio, who had some difficulty in reaching the highest ones but employed a thin stick with a crook in it for the purpose, had each succeeded in quarter filling their baskets. Wanda had less and my basket had only about half a dozen shoots in it. I was consumed with envy, which I did my best to conceal. Nevertheless, insubstantial though they appeared, these *asparagi selvatici*, when boiled until tender and then eaten cold rather than hot with vinaigrette dressing, were delicious.

When the time came for us to go back to England, Attilio's farewell offering was very acceptable but difficult to deal with: a great earthenware jar that looked as if it had been dug up at Luni that contained the entire olive oil harvest of I Castagni for the previous year which had been pressed at the *frantoio* at Caniparola. Even after giving him a generous quantity it had been difficult to find any containers at this late stage to transport it in; but eventually we found some plastic containers that were sufficiently large. Signora Angiolina's gift to us was a vast bottle of red wine, which was equally difficult to find room for.

We left for England at five in the morning when the sun was just beginning to shoot up behind the Apuan Alps. It was going to be a wonderful day, even the radio said so, something spring days had mostly been able to avoid being up to now. The vines in our *vigneto* had already begun to sprout small shoots.

When we went to say goodbye to the Dadà, Tranquillo had

already left for the woods but Rina was there, looking more like Artemis than ever, to see us off, give us lots of hot coffee to fortify us for the journey to Le Havre and gifts of *salsa di pomodoro* and *pesto*.

'Come back soon,' she said. 'Don't forget us.' It was the nicest thing anyone could say to us.

Chapter Eleven

IT WAS NOT UNTIL the end of September that we were able to return to I Castagni, just a few days before the *vendemmia* was due to begin. Usually, the grapes in these parts were not ready to be picked any earlier than this. The *vendemmia* began after the Festa di San Remigio which took place on 1 October, the saint who had baptized Clovis, King of the Franks, and whose effigy looked down on everyone a trifle severely from high above the altar in the church in Fosdinovo. It was said that it always rained on the Festa di San Remigio.

One important piece of local news was that Rina's baby was due the following spring. It turned out to be a fine boy who was christened Michele. In spite of this she still contrived to milk Bionda, her cow, almost until the moment of his arrival.

The other was that ever since we left for England Signora Angiolina's sister and brother-in-law had been living with her. During this time they had managed to have a house built next door to Signora Angiolina's place. This seemed like some sort of record as it had not even been started when we left for home, although it was not completely ready for occupation.

It was a single-storey building with four rooms including a kitchen and a bathroom, an almost unheard of luxury then that few people actually made use of, even if they possessed one, and it had an ample veranda which sheltered it from the sun and from which the passing traffic could be observed, altogether an ideal place for a pair of *pensionati* such as Signor and Signora Tarsiero.

Signora Fernanda, Signora Angiolina's sister, was at that time still dark-haired and very, very thin. Her husband, Signor Giuseppe, was a handsome man with a fine head of grey hair and an impressive Roman nose. He looked like a better sort of Roman senator. Both he and his wife were still full of energy. They had needed to be to get a house built in six months; but in fact they had already got permission to build it long before we arrived on the scene.

Both Signor Giuseppe and Signora Fernanda had spent many years of their lives cultivating fruit and vegetables and a large vineyard for some landlords at a place called Pagazzana in the valley of the Magra, beyond Sarzana. It had been a hard life and they had worked like Trojans. Now they had retired.

Signora Fernanda's favourite expression, the equivalent to her sister's '*Hai fatto bene!*' was '*mosca!*' which in Italian means either 'fly!' or 'Moscow!', depending on whether the 'm' is a capital or not. When Wanda asked her what she meant when she used it, was it *Mosca!* or *mosca!*, she said *mosca!* with a small 'm'. No, she couldn't remember where she learnt it but it was long ago, when she was a young girl.

When Signora Fernanda was going flat out in the conversation game, and she spoke rather rapidly, we both used to try and guess when '*mosca!*' might come up. It was a bit like playing roulette. 'Now!' Wanda used to say in English to avoid hurting the Signora's feelings; but it never did come up at that moment. Sometimes it didn't come up for ages, which made it even more welcome when it did.

Signor Giuseppe had a good singing voice which he used to exercise on his way down the hill to visit us at I Castagni. He also wrote poetry, poems about the arcadian beauty of the woods which surrounded us and the general salubriousness of the place.

One, rather surprisingly for a man of the Left, was addressed to the Madonna.

97

Preghiera di	Prayer of an old man
un vecchio alla nostra	to Our Madonna
Signora degli Angeli	of the Angels
Cara Madonna mia	Dear Madonna
non mi mandare via.	don't send me away.
Sono vecchio	I am old
non c'è la faccio più	I can't go on
di lavorare.	working any more.
Ma qualcosa di buono	But I can still do
so sempre fare.	something good.
C'è tanta gioventù	There are so many young people
che la terra non vuol	who don't want to work
lavorare più.	on the land any more.
C'è tanta gente che	But there are still people
ha ancora voglia di lavorare	who want to work
ma senza compassione	but are treated
nelle fabbriche	without compassion
si vede trattare.	in the factories.
Lo so che in questo mondo	I know that in this world
si sta male	one doesn't live well
ma al di là	but over the Jordan
peggio si starà	without friends
e senza compagnia.	it will be even worse.
Cara Madonna mia	Dear Madonna
non mi mandare via.	don't send me away.

We always used to look forward to listening to Signor Giuseppe reciting his poems. He made the world about us seem and sound good, much better than when he went on, as he sometimes did, about the State of the Nation, about which he had strong feelings; 'the Nation' being Italy and the Italians. Listening to him on this subject always left me wondering how Italy could survive at all and why, in spite of doing all the wrong things economically and not paying tax on a grand scale, Italians not only seemed to enjoy themselves more than we did but appeared to live better, in everyday terms, than we did.

Signora Angiolina was very happy that they had come to live next door. Now Signor Giuseppe would be able to take over her vineyard which her husband had planted but which was now showing signs of neglect. This was also good for Signor Giuseppe who otherwise would have to start one from scratch.

We too were happy at the thought of Signor Giuseppe arriving amongst us. We badly needed his advice about what we should do with our own vineyard. The whole property required a lot of new vines and these would have to be planted in fresh soil that had not had vines growing in it for many years, otherwise, we were told, they wouldn't flourish.

I would have liked to have asked Attilio to take over the job of tending the vines but, Leonardo da Vincean genius though he might be in so many fields, the making of drinkable wine was another of the few skills that seemed to have escaped him. That is if some of the wines he had made at I Castagni were anything to go by. When Attilio opened a bottle of wine of his own production strange unidentifiable things sometimes used to come to the surface, as I remembered them surfacing when, as a sailor many years previously, I had passed through the Sargasso Sea. However, we could hardly complain. In our absence he had cut up a whole lot more wood we had got from Tranquillo the previous Easter, into more burnable lengths.

I was pleased and proud to be liked by Attilio; but the one he was really devoted to was Wanda. This was partly because whenever possible she used to ask him his opinion on important matters connected with the property, which probably no one had ever done before, and partly because she was always giving him things to repair and he loved mending things. The modern idea of 'replacing the unit' if anything broke would have been as repugnant to Attilio as it was to Wanda.

To carry out these repairs he used to retire to the 'secret' room for hours at a time where he could be heard chuckling to himself as he worked away and carrying on all sorts of what would have been fascinating conversations with himself if only anyone else had been able to hear what he was saying. Now, of course, they could be taped. Once he repaired a large English ceramic meat dish that had broken into three pieces, using iron rivets. Often he went away to do *giornate*; but when either of us asked him whether things had gone well his invariable answer was '*Non c'è male*', 'Not too bad'. And with that one had to be content. But he did tell us some of his stories. We used to invite him to sit by the fire in the evenings with a few glasses of wine, which he really enjoyed. He told them with his eyes closed: the wonderful adventures of the Green Seaweed Man and so on.

Now for the first time, the house began to look like a house, albeit a rather battered one, less like a Stone Age fort. It now had a roof, or rather a number of roofs, and the windows had glass in them and were fitted with shutters, instead of being gaping holes in the masonry; but there were still more windows for me to excavate in these walls, and I started work on them with a hammer and chisel.

Attilio made another memorable contribution to the rehabilitation of I Castagni while we were away. With the aid of another old and almost equally diminutive man called Dadà Settimo, a member of another ramification of the Dadà family, and a seventh son, hence his name, he built a splendid pergola on to the front of the house where the bread oven was, using timber left over from what we had bought at the *demolizioni*. They had then planted it with creeping vines which were now clambering up it at a tremendous rate. This meant that, if all went well, we would soon be able to eat outside in the middle of the day which at the moment was impossible in the hot weather because of the absence of shade.

Dadà Settimo and his wife lived in a little house on the edge of the next bend on the main road going up to Fosdinovo, high up on the far side of the torrent from us. He had been in the Alpini in the First War and had fought against the Austro-Hungarians in the Alps. He had a small black moustache, always wore his Alpini hat and looked the absolute model of an Alpino. He used to attend Alpini reunions at which, he said, some pretty tough drinking used to take place.

He and his wife had a married daughter, Signora Maria, whose husband, Signor Marchini Orfeo, worked in the naval dockyard at La Spezia. Orfeo had also been a member of the Alpini in the Second World War and had gone to Russia with the Divisione Giulia. He had been one of the comparatively few to survive the Russian winter and return home relatively unscathed.

Countless Italian soldiers had died in the Steppes because they were appallingly badly equipped – instead of being issued with thick stockings and lined boots to wear in mid-winter they had been given pieces of cloth to wind round their feet. The majority were never heard of again.

Orfeo was a gentle person, nothing like one imagined an ex-Alpino who had fought in Russia in winter would be. He had been a driver with, eventually, nothing to drive when temperatures plummeted way below zero. When he smiled the smile used to break slowly over his face. It was like the sunrise coming.

The Marchinis had a grown-up daughter; all five of them – Marchinis and Dadà – lived in the house. It was difficult to imagine how they contrived to do so but they did. We saw a lot of them, except the old lady, Settimo's wife, who was ill and rarely appeared. Their property was linked to ours by a labyrinth of paths so that, when they were working in one of their minute fields, they were doing so immediately overhead and we could carry on a conversation with them at the same time. Sometimes in the evenings we used to drop in on them. When we did I talked to Signor Settimo and Signor Orfeo about war, and Wanda talked to Signora Maria, who was dark and very thin and had bad eyesight – most people were thin in these hills – about how to grow roses. Everyone was interested in her Queen Elizabeths – a subject about which almost everyone in the neighbourhood was ignorant, as they were of most other kinds of ornamental gardening. And sometimes we would stay to dinner.

In fact we didn't visit Signor Orfeo and Signora Maria as much as we would have liked to have done because every time we did so they loaded us with wine and vegetables, and at that time we had not got all that much to reciprocate with.

Eventually, the bringing of presents from England for all these various families became a major preoccupation, involving a complicated protocol. There were lots of people and families to visit now. And quite a number of these were beginning to visit us, sometimes doing so quite deliberately when we were not at home, leaving behind them some offering, and making us rack our brains to try and guess who it had been.

Now there was mist in the early mornings and the vines were heavy with grapes, even our own in their ancient *pergole*.

It was interesting. With all the evidence that we eventually accumulated over many years there seemed to be no doubt to us that I Castagni was a place with a remarkable resistance to decay. One in which things, whether they were doors, or vines, or main beams such as the one the adder cast his or her skin on with such regularity, or whatever they were, teetered on the verge of collapse but never collapsed completely.

And now it was, in the late afternoons, together again after having been separated for so long, that Signora Angiolina and Signora Fernanda could be seen and heard coming down the hill and over the torrent, bone-dry now, to the front door of I Castagni, armed with their sickles to cut what grass and alfalfa there still was to feed their rabbits.

And when they had cut enough and bundled it up in their aprons, they used to plonk themselves down on the stone seat below the oven and have long conversations with Wanda, which always began '*Ma sa com'è*, Signora Wanda' ('But you know how it is, Signora Wanda'), or '*Ma senta un po*', Signora Wanda' ('But listen a bit, Signora Wanda'), before getting down to the sometimes gory details of what was going on in the locality. What they never did, ever, nor any of the other ladies in the area, was speak badly of their immediate neighbours.

And then Wanda would ask them if they would like a cup of tea and Signora Angiolina would accept and Signora Fernanda would hold up her hands in total prohibition, as if it was some sort of deadly poison she was being offered, at the same time saying, '*Non lo voglio*' ('I don't want it'), only to drink it when it finally appeared.

Sometimes Signora Fernanda took us to visit the present occupants of Il Posticcio, a house of the Malaspina in which she and Signora Angiolina had lived when they had been girls. This strangely named house, Posticcio, signifying Sham, was a large and tall house with a turret rising from one corner of it which gave it a mediaeval aspect. In fact, it probably was mediaeval. Inside the entrance door there was a huge, now-decayed room with a big, gaping fireplace at one end, and upstairs there was a labyrinth of rooms, some of them very small and under the eaves. It was the sort of house from which I imagined Don Quixote setting out on his travels, accompanied by Sancho Panza. Outside, what had been the *vigneto* was so overgrown with brambles and blackberry bushes that it was difficult to believe that it had, at one time, produced the best red wine in the area.

One afternoon Signora Fernanda came down to the house alone, ostensibly to cut some alfalfa and have the usual chat. This time it was still going to be a chat, but one of a rather different kind. Signora Angiolina, finding herself too timid to tell us the secrets of her life, the ones she had promised to tell, now sent her sister to impart them to us. There was no obligation for Signora Angiolina to unburden herself in this way or for Signora Fernanda to act the part of the messenger but this is what they had decided to do.

'I must tell you,' Signora Fernanda said, after some general preamble, 'that Angiolina was a very beautiful girl and had innumerable admirers, all of whom had their heads turned if she even looked in their direction.

'Partly because of this, our parents thought it would be better she became engaged when she was still very young, about seventeen, to a local boy about a year older than she was. This was when we lived in Il Posticcio over the hill below the Dadà place.

'Now she had this *fidanzato*, a nice, serious boy but not old enough, or experienced enough, you know, Signora, to protect Angiolina as she needed to be protected.

'For there was another, a man five or six years older than she was, a man of violent passion, and when she became betrothed and he realized that my sister would never be his, he made the decision to destroy them both.

'His opportunity came when my sister and her *fidanzato* went to a *ballo liscio* [literally a "smooth dance"], a dance on a shiny wooden floor, usually in summer in the open air, for which we used to buy tickets. A sort of dance that used to be very popular, and still is in some places, although now thought to be rather old-fashioned.

'There, as Angiolina and her *fidanzato* were dancing together, he took out a pistol and first shot her *fidanzato* dead and then shot Angiolina, the bullet passing so close to her heart that she was lucky to survive.'

'What happened to him, the man who shot them?' Wanda asked.

'He was sent to prison,' Signora Fernanda said, 'for three or four years, I can't remember now how long. It was not for very long because it was what we call here *un delitto di passione*, a crime of passion, not a murder.'

It sounded pretty premeditated to me.

'But that was not the end of it,' Signora Fernanda continued. 'Somehow the news of this *delitto* got into the newspapers in New York and as a result Angiolina received a number of offers of marriage from Italians living there; but she never replied to any of them.'

'What happened then?' Wanda asked.

'Three years later she married a local man, a few years older than she was. He was a good man.'

✠

Almost every day Signor Giuseppe used to take off from his new house up the hill where he was getting ready to do Signora Angiolina's *vendemmia* and come down the hill to our dell, singing a bit on the way. This was what most men did when visiting or passing through other people's properties by the labyrinth of tracks and paths that were normally open to anyone who wished to use them, except uninvited *cacciatori*. Women would cough discreetly or carry on an over-loud conversation with who-ever they were travelling with.

These footpaths were an important part of the rural economy and had been since time immemorial. Without them the whole system of intercommunication on the hillside would have come to a halt. One reason for all this ceremony – the coughing and the singing – was probably so as not to catch the owners of these properties with their trousers down or their skirts up, or both, something that did happen in the course of the long, hot after-noons.

When Signor Giuseppe did come it was invariably to bring with him some useful offering, or to give us some useful piece of advice, such as pointing out some defect in the building that had not yet been made good, but ought to have been.

It was at this time, soon after we had arrived, that he decided that the trunk of a small chestnut tree that had been used as a newly installed beam to support the tiled roof over the staircase that led up to the upper floor at the front of the building was too thin at one end to perform this function satisfactorily. What was needed was a real, rectangular beam of the sort we had bought from the *demolizioni*.

The tree trunk had been set up by Alberto and Renato who fre-quently joined forces in order to carry out some particular piece of work more easily. The reason why they hadn't used a beam from the *demolizioni* was that they had used up all the long ones and didn't relish going all the way back there to get another. In the circumstances, I would have done the same thing. The only persons Signor Giuseppe expressed his fears to were Wanda and myself. He never said anything either to Alberto or Renato, but in order to draw attention to its fragility – the trunk certainly was rather thin at one end – he found a well-seasoned piece of timber about five feet high which he painted an unsuitable shade of pale blue so that it would show up nicely and then wedged it vertically under the trunk at the thin end which helped to take some of the weight off it.

If either of us had done such a thing, or even suggested that the trunk might be insufficiently strong at one end to do the job, then both Alberto and Renato might well have decided to down tools and walk off the site; although by now we were on such friendly terms, particularly with Renato and his family, that such a happening was unlikely.

It was only because Signor Giuseppe was a local man, born in the neighbourhood (even the years spent at Pagazzana didn't count against him), married to a local woman, Signora Fernanda, and an *esperto* in all sorts of things, including vine-growing and wine-producing, that he was able to get away with it.

In fact, the thin end of the tree never gave the slightest cause for alarm, although what would have happened to it if Signor Giuseppe's pale blue baulk had not been put in to relieve the strain, we shall now never know. Nevertheless Renato went on for years and years about the solidity of the thin end, every time he was on the premises.

✛

It was during another of Signor Giuseppe's visits that a really awful rustic mishap occurred.

He had got it into his head that our well needed cleaning out and being a countryman saw nothing strange in arriving on our doorstep at half-past six in the morning to discuss the matter, without telling us that he was coming and without the usual premonitory arias. He was, therefore, at the front door before Wanda espied him. She was already in the kitchen – she likes getting up early – heating up the basic ingredients for a soup. I was still asleep in the bedroom overhead.

'ERIC. E VENUTO IL SIGNOR GIUSEPPE!' she cried in her best Slovenian banshee voice.

Leaping to my feet in answer to this cry I managed to get one foot out of the bedclothes but then, instead of placing it on the floor, succeeded in plunging it into what was now a more than half-full *vaso da notte*, turning it over in the process. We had installed it in the bedroom in order to avoid making a journey down the front steps in the open air to what was now the bathroom; and it was with horror that I watched its contents flow down through the gaps in the floor planking, part of it, it transpired, on to the head of Signor Giuseppe which was now perfectly sited down below in the kitchen to receive it, and part of it into Wanda's soup which was bubbling away in a vessel on the stove.

It was fortunate that Signor Giuseppe never discovered what he had been anointed with. I told him that it was clean water from a wash basin that I had overturned, and he appeared to be content with this explanation. Wanda, on the other hand, who had had her dish defiled and was under no illusions as to what it was, was less contented. She didn't speak to me for the rest of the day, which was soupless.

☩

Sometimes in these late September days quite suddenly the sky clouded over and the thunder rumbled behind the peaks and those who had vines prayed that they would be spared the hail, which could destroy an entire crop of grapes in a matter of minutes at this time of year. And at night the terraces around the house were alive with bats, and sometimes there were fireflies floating among the vines, looking like illuminated galleons floating in a sea of darkness.

We were happy at I Castagni.

Chapter Twelve

THAT YEAR, WANDA was buying an ox-tongue from the shop up at Fosdinovo when the Signora asked her if she would be prepared to act as a waitress, for the midday meal in the restaurant at the hotel on the day of the Festa di San Remigio. Apparently she always laid on a special lunch for the farmers and their wives on that day when they came in from the country to attend the *festa* and because the prices were very reasonable and the food was good it was always a great success.

The problem was that it was becoming increasingly difficult to recruit extra waitresses. This year, the Signora said, she was desperate. Two of her best girls, sisters, had been taken ill with flu and were unable to come. All she now had left were her daughters, the ones we had accompanied on the procession, and one of them would probably be needed to work in the bar. Her husband would help but would probably be needed in the bar, too.

'What do you think?' Wanda asked me. 'Should I do it? I don't have to wear a uniform, or anything.'

'I think you should do it, that is if you want to,' I said. 'I'm not sure about not wearing a uniform or anything, with a lot of gentlemen about; but you might get some tips. You might even get a proposal from some lonely farmer.' At the time I thought I was joking. So Wanda said she would do it.

Meanwhile the preparations for the *vendemmia* in Lunigiana and in every other part of northern Italy where grapes grew were approaching a climax. Now every wine-growing property, however small, had its barrels, standing outside the cellars in the open where they had been scrubbed and washed and kept standing upright with a hose running water into them until the staves swelled sufficiently to ensure that they didn't leak. Uncountable thousands of gallons of water were consumed in this way. We had done the same with the two modest barrels that we had inherited with I Castagni, one for red, the other for white, following the instructions of Signor Giuseppe.

And throughout the surrounding countryside, and in the nearby towns and villages, relatives and friends were recruited to take part in the picking of the grapes and the crushing of them and the pressing of them. And wherever a quorum of *contadini* came together the talk was of nothing but the *vendemmia*.

And every specialist shop in Sarzana, Fosdinovo and along the dreadful traffic-ridden Via Aurelia towards Carrara had most of their stock out on the pavements: barrels, some of them enormous; *bigonci*, heavy wooden tubs used to carry the grapes to the grape crusher, which now performed the function until recently performed by human feet; the presses; the apparatus used to cork the bottles; and demijohns, and other receptacles of all sorts of shapes and sizes, sometimes straw-covered, more often now covered with plastic.

And there were corks, wooden bungs, funnels, secateurs, *olio enologico*, the special odourless oil used to protect the wine in the demijohn from the air, and pipettes to draw the oil off, and metal caps for the demijohns to foil the local mice, which had the peculiar habit of eating their way through plastic ones, then dipping their tails in the oil and sucking them, until all the oil had been consumed, leaving the wine free to go off.

And there were all sorts of chemicals on sale, used to clarify white wine, and to prevent it changing colour when it was sent elsewhere, to England for instance, an overdose of which renders the wine as unnaturally pallid as water and gives whoever drinks it a fearful headache between the eyes.

✝

It was a fine and sunny day for the *festa*, a day on which, according to the inhabitants of Fosdinovo, any day could be called a good day providing it wasn't coming down in buckets; but this was a really wonderful one, a day to remember.

Long before dawn we were woken by what sounded like an armoured division on the move, the noise made by an almost interminable procession of heavily laden vans, lorries and cars groaning up through the last nineteen or so bends head to tail to Fosdinovo. Normally all we heard down in our dell at I Castagni in the way of loud noises was when the driver of the bus between Sarzana and Fosdinovo, or vice versa, pulled out all the stops on what were the modern equivalent of motor horns, which he did every time he entered one of the hairpins. This was something he would continue to do, and his successors would continue to do, three or four times a day for the next twenty-five or so years, and are still doing.

The market was set up in a large, open space shaded by magnificent plane trees below the ramparts at the lower end of the town. It took hours for these market people to unload all the merchandise from their vehicles and set it up on the stalls. It was difficult to imagine anyone unpacking, for example, several hundred pairs of shoes, setting them out on a stall and then, a few hours later, packing the whole lot up again; but this is what the market people did, six or even seven days a week. For them every day was a *festa*. Normally they didn't enjoy the Festa di San Remigio because of the effect it had on the weather. Today they were happy. The only one who wasn't was a man with a stall full of umbrellas.

It would be nice to pretend otherwise but even then, back in the 1960s, the great majority of what was on offer was cheap, mass-produced stuff, and one would have had to go back another ten or fifteen years in time to find anything different. But nevertheless artifacts of an Attilian, pre-plastic age were still on sale, and some of them still are on sale in markets all over Italy to this day.

Here, if you were in the mood, you could buy rope, chains, pack-saddles, harness, whips made from bulls' pizzles, shepherds' crooks, sheep and cattle bells, butter churns, axes, all sorts of knives, cross-cut saws (chain saws were still not in general use in these parts), the sort of hand saws Attilio made, in which the tension of the blade was maintained with a twisted cord, the wooden shovels used in bread ovens, scythes, reaping hooks, various sorts of bill hooks which varied in shape from region to region, *rotelline* (small, toothed wheels with wooden handles used for cutting certain kinds of pasta), hand-knitted socks and vests with the natural grease still in the wool, corduroy trousers robust enough to stand up by themselves without anyone in them, clogs, and mountain boots.

And there were mousetraps, the sort Attilio made, and casseroles, and copper cauldrons. And there were *preti*, priests – wooden frameworks put between the sheets on cold winter nights with iron pots full of hot ashes inside them which warmed a bed more thoroughly than any other sort of warmer, and could also quite easily burn the house down while doing so, as they not infrequently used to when almost every family had one.

But most of the real business was being done at the stalls which dealt in less rustic objects, which made up the majority of what was on sale. In *indumenti intimi*, otherwise women's underwear, where ladies, some of them pretty generously designed, were measuring what looked like being rather inadequate knickers against their thighs; in *residui di guerra*, otherwise army surplus, where you could buy old gas mask cases and genuine imitation leather Flying Fortress jackets with imitation sheepskin linings; while on the LP record stalls people were stocking up on Ornella Vanoni belting 'I Giorni dell' Amore' and Mongo Santamaria doing 'Water Melon Man', which, mingled with the cries of a couple of hundred stallholders all inviting the customers to close in and buy, made a fine old din.

And there was also a brisk trade being done in what appeared to be highly dangerous gas balloons which adventurous grandmothers were snapping up for their grandchildren. An expensive way of sending the little darlings on a trip to eternity.

A short distance down the side of the hill towards Monte della

Forca, a place where the Malaspina used to operate a gallows, there was an open space under the trees in which the cattle market was taking place. In it pigs and mules and sheep and cows were changing hands, the potential buyers squatting on their haunches while the owners, hard-looking men, dealt with them by way of *mediatori*. Occasionally, one of these sellers would mount a horse and trot it up the road and back for a bit to show off its paces. Most of the buying and selling was already finished. It had taken place as soon as the animals had been led down into the market from the various lorries and loose boxes in which they had been brought here, but as one old man said at the drinking booth, 'Every year the sales are diminishing here at Fosdinovo, and every year more animals are left unsold; but nevertheless people will still bring their animals to be sold here and will do so for a long time yet because they enjoy buying and selling, and the day.'

Meanwhile, up in the town of Fosdinovo, in the Church of San Remigio, the bells were clanging away, summoning those of the faithful who were not still in search of over-sized knickers or Flying Fortress jackets with imitation sheepskin linings, or had not yet started looking for them, to attend a high mass celebrated by the Bishop of Massa, or it could have been Carrara, we were never quite sure. This was the most important of the three masses that were celebrated at Fosdinovo on the Festa di San Remigio, in the course of which enough incense would be ejected from their thuribles to satisfy the most profligate of acolytes. It was a happy scene that confronted me down there in the market place – Wanda had already gone off, not without a certain amount of apprehension, to be instructed by the Signora in her waitressing duties – the sun shone down through the leaves on the plane trees which were oscillating in the light breeze that was blowing, filling the market place with tremulous light and shade so that it, and its now almost innumerable occupants, looked as if they were at the bottom of the sea.

Down here in the market there was plenty to eat and drink. There were booths under the trees, furnished with long trestle tables with white cloths on them, at which uncannily look-alike farmers, all wearing suits and felt hats and waistcoats with watch chains, sat drinking either *vino bianco* or *nero*, munching *panini*, sandwiches made at the table with the local *mortadella* or *salami*, and all having animated conversations about the state of the nation, the coming *vendemmia* which, apparently, was not going to be too bad, and who had run away with whom – one being a priest who had done a bunk with his housekeeper – I couldn't hear where this had taken place. Otherwise they talked about the weather.

If you wanted the ultimate in *panini* you went to a stall across the way from the booths where a man and his wife made them to order – with crusty homemade bread, filled with pork cut from a *porchetta*, a suckling pig, peppered and stuffed with garlic and herbs, that had been roasted on a spit, delicious, very expensive and very rich.

Armed with one of these *panini di porchetta*, I ordered half a litre of *vino nero*, joined the company at one of the tables and waited for them to come up with the next subject. What would it be, the Beatles, birth control? No one spoke to me, apart from saying, '*Buon giorno,*' in a friendly way. It was incredibly restful down here under the trees. Rather as I imagined Wodehouse's Drones Club might have been. Disappointingly, when they did start to talk, it was about football.

Here, everyone was drinking last year's wine, decent but unremarkable, as most people said this year's would be. Here, too often in early autumn it rained and rained when the *scirocco* blew from Africa, and then the grapes began to suffer from mildew. Here, in an area which only appeared on the most optimistic wine maps as being of moderate wine production, it was rare to have an outstanding year. Here, the farmers made white and red wine – the red was better – using as many varieties of grapes as possible.

This wine was rarely, if ever, on sale to the public. When farmers sold what was surplus to their own enormous needs, it invariably found its way into the houses of friends and acquaintances or else into the sort of *trattoria* which announces that its cooking is *cucina casalinga*. But not any *trattoria*, however good the cooking. Of the four we had so far patronized in the area, all recommended by local people, only one served wine that had not been *lavorato*, mucked about with. This was not because the proprietors of the other three were dishonest; but because there wasn't enough of the wine that hadn't been mucked about with to go around, after the producers had had a go at it.

It was mid-afternoon when Wanda finally appeared, tired but happy. She had really enjoyed herself. 'I haven't worked so hard for years,' she said. 'People started to arrive at about half-past eleven and by *mezzogiorno* the place was full. There must have been fifty people sitting down, most of them men, most of them farmers, not many women. And there was a queue of about twenty all the way up the stairs, waiting for tables. They were going to have a long wait, so the Signora said that they should come back at half-past one and that she would keep some tables for them. Some went down to the bar and had a glass of wine and a *panino* to keep them going.

'The Signora's mother did the cooking, helped by the Signora who had to keep on going back to her shop for fresh supplies. Her husband and one of her daughters worked in the bar and when he had a moment he acted as a waiter. The other sister worked as a waitress and did all the bills which was a great help. And I didn't have to do the washing up.

'The food was very good. There was a choice of *antipasti*, the usual things, and *pasta al forno*, and roast veal, pork chops, stewed tripe, all with roast potatoes, and ended with jam pastry, and all sorts of fruit. And there was lots of wine.

'The farmers were lovely. Some of them said it was the first time they had a foreign waitress serving them food. I said I wasn't as foreign as they thought and that I had been brought up at Fontanellato near Parma and I gave them a bit of *dialetto parmigiano* to be getting on with. They all left me tips but I left them for the regulars.

'You know you made a joke about marrying a farmer?' she went on. 'Well, one of them asked me to marry him. He was very

nice, very correct, a widower, about fifty, with a whitish moustache.'

'What did you say?' I asked. 'I can always grow a moustache,
probably even a whitish one. I didn't think you liked them.'

'I said I can't marry you just now,' she said. 'So he said he
would ask me again next year.'

'And what did you say to that?' I asked.

'I said, all right, you can ask me.'

'Will you do it again next year?' I asked, genuinely impressed
at the thought of having a rival for her hand in his fifties and with
a whitish moustache.

'I will,' she said, almost pertly, 'if they ask me.'

'If things go on like this,' I said, 'I can see myself growing a
whitish moustache and going to an agricultural college to learn
farm management, trying to catch up with this man.' But she
wasn't listening.

'Then, when it was all over and all the guests had gone away
we all sat down, the staff that is, and had an enormous lunch.

'Just before I was leaving to come here,' Wanda said, 'the
Signora took me to one side and asked me if I was still interested
in getting some beds for our house. Apparently, she and her husband have been told that their hotel is too old-fashioned and that
if they don't do something about it pretty quickly they will be
downgraded. So they have decided to modernize it and the first
thing they're going to do is to get rid of some of the beds and a
lot of other furniture.'

'But the furniture's marvellous, not grand but very nice, and so
are the beds, at least the ones I've seen are. They must be mad,' I
said.

'It's not they who are mad, it's the Tourist people,' said
Wanda. 'And marvellous or not, according to the Signora they're
going to have difficulty in even giving it away. She had a man up
from Sarzana to look at it, and he wasn't interested.

'She took me up to an attic. Most of the beds she wants to get
rid of are up there in the dark but she had a torch. There's a beautiful mahogany one, like a *chaise-longue*, made in Lucca; but she

115

doesn't want to get rid of that. Anyway it's too good for I Castagni. There are some wonderful iron ones and there are some of those decorated with mother-of-pearl designs and some have little oval paintings of country scenes. And they all have mattresses, all very clean. They looked as if they'd just been renewed. One of the beds I really like hasn't any springs but the Signora said that she knows someone in Sarzana who can make some up for us.

'Altogether I chose five, two singles for the front bedroom upstairs, a double for us at the back and two singles for the loft upstairs.'

'Do you think we can afford all these beds?' I asked. 'Won't they be too expensive?'

'She's only asking 40,000 lire,' said Wanda, 'and she's letting us have a kitchen table as well.'

Chapter Thirteen

WE CARRIED OUT our first *vendemmia* at I Castagni a couple of days after the Festa di San Remigio, with the help of Signor Giuseppe and Signora Fernanda, who proved surprisingly agile, and with Signora Angiolina giving us encouragement from the sidelines. We were lucky to have Signor Giuseppe to show us how it should be done. Although I knew how to drink it, I only had a rudimentary idea of how wine was made.

Signor Giuseppe had already done Signora Angiolina's *vendemmia*, having taken over the responsibility for it, much to her relief.

We had been told that Signor Giuseppe always did his *vendemmia* long before anyone else but this year, with the weather apparently set fair, local people said he would have been well advised to have waited another week; but he was anxious to get it over and done with. It is possible that this determination to get the wine, as it were, stowed away, safely under the hatches, was because at one time he had had some unfortunate experience with the dreaded hail or some other natural disaster, when he was working for the proprietors of the big vineyard down in the plain.

When he came to our *vendemmia* he was equally impatient for us to get it done; but although we realized that it was too early we did our best to carry it out as efficiently as possible, setting up a table on which we sifted out the good grapes from the not-so-good and those that were just awful.

Those that were the most difficult to get rid of and were particularly hostile to the making of good wine were pale green,

117

about half the size of a pea and as hard as rock. No sun, however hot, would ever ripen them.

Some of our vines, especially those bearing red grapes, were very old with very thick stems like miniature stunted trees; but although everyone prophesied their immediate demise they, like everything else at I Castagni, continued to flourish for another quarter of a century and were still doing so when we left.

Signor Giuseppe was not interested in sorting tables or anything effeminate like that. He liked to put everything, apart from stalks, into the squashing machine, believing, as he said, that the preponderance of good grapes would nullify the effects of those that were not so good.

'*Via!*' ('Away with them!') he would say, making a gesture of dismissal with one hand as he allowed some discussable grapes to be engulfed by the machine, a bit like a monarch ordering the decapitation of some recalcitrant subjects, while at the same time, on a whim, allowing others to go free.

In fact, from now on, it became an unacknowledged struggle between Signor Giuseppe and ourselves, on his part not to omit a single grape, if possible sweeping them off the sifting table before Wanda and Signora Fernanda had a chance to go through any kind of selection, on our part to thwart him; but we always needed his help.

The machine which Signor Giuseppe lent us for our *vendemmia*, and continued to lend us for all the years we lived at I Castagni, was really the property of Signora Angiolina. It looked like a wheelbarrow but with a pair of carrying handles in lieu of wheels. It was made of galvanized iron and it had a rectangular hole in the bottom of it in which a horizontal screw similar to those that mince the meat in a sausage machine was turned by a handle. Larger, more sophisticated versions were operated by electricity.

When it was to be used – it took two people to operate it effectively – it was lowered on to one of the *bigonci*. Then while one person kept it topped up with grapes, the other turned the handle and crushed them and they were precipitated into the *bigoncio*, juice, skins, pips, stalks and all, although serious efforts were made to cut off as many of the heaviest stalks as possible while the bunches were being gathered.

Then, when the *bigoncio* was almost full, the two operators lifted the machine off the *bigoncio*, using the carrying handles, and set it down on another, empty *bigoncio*, and the whole process was repeated.

Then the strongest of the two operators, which virtually meant one who had not yet suffered a hernia, and most males of middle age in this community had suffered one, with the help of his colleague hoisted the filled *bigoncio* on to one of his shoulders and he then poured the contents into one of the oak barrels which were raised off the ground on wooden platforms.

All we had to do now was to wait for the fermentation to begin. When it did, it was heralded by the appearance of innumerable minute insects which hovered above what were now the seething contents of the barrels, which had either given birth to them or inspired them to appear; and eventually they disappeared as suddenly as they had come. From time to time during this period, exhorted by Signor Giuseppe to do so, I pushed a wooden pole up and down in what is called the *mosto* to accelerate the process of fermentation.

Then one morning after about ten days had passed, Signor Giuseppe loosened the wooden bung on the barrel that contained the red grapes and what looked like a great gush of blood poured out of it and began to fill the *bigonci* we had ready for this moment at a tremendous rate. From them we transferred the wine into demijohns, topping them up with *olio enologico* when the wine reached the neck to stop the air getting to the wine. We then capped them with wired-on metal caps to foil the dreaded mice.

This was the moment, when the wine came gushing out of the barrel, when we each took a glass of the new wine and drank it, still foaming, and this was the moment when Signor Giuseppe always said, '*Questo vino è una cannonata! Un vino genuino!*' And both Signora Angiolina and Signora Fernanda, and Wanda and myself would all concur.

'What do you really think of it?' I asked Wanda the first time.

'I think it's pretty awful; but then I don't like new wine. I think it will be all right,' she said, 'providing it doesn't go on tasting like this.'

'Well, what do you think it tastes of?' I said.

'I think,' she said, 'that it tastes of old rusty nuts and bolts, like Teran [the local red wine in her particular part of Slovenia]; but then Teran is very good with food.'

Whatever the taste, for us it was an historic moment. We had made our first wine!

Of the two, the white seemed slightly better than the red, but eventually, when we began to drink them the following year, the red turned out to be really quite good, with only a few hints of nuts and bolts. The white was not so good and we didn't improve it by adding too much bisulphite, which we were told would prevent it assuming a brownish colour when we took it to England. It stopped it changing colour but produced a rather sickly drink that gave us a nasty pain between the eyes.

Now Signor Giuseppe put a couple of wedges under the back of the barrel so that the last of the wine could be drained into a *bigoncio*. This was the last of the free-run wine, what we then hoped would be the *vino buono*. What now remained in the barrels were the skins, the pips, those stalks that had not been cut off when the grapes were picked, and those tiny, green, iron-hard grapes that had either escaped detection at the sorting table or else had been too numerous to deal with, about which nothing could be done any more, and a lot of wine still in the skins, to be extracted by pressing.

Now the first of the two barrels was turned on its side and with our bare hands we dug out of it what looked like a red sludge and put it in the press, which had been got ready for the purpose. It, too, was the property of Signora Angiolina and was about the smallest of its kind available.

Signora Angiolina's press was really a barrel with loose-fitting staves and a loose-fitting lid raised on a wooden platform. It was constructed in such a way that when it was filled with what was left of the grapes after the crushing process and a screw was operated by turning a capstan bar on the top of the instrument, the lid was forced down on the contents squeezing out the wine so that it flowed through the gaps between the staves, and down through channels carved in the wooden platform on which it stood and into a receptacle below it. To squeeze all the wine out required several pressings. After each one wooden blocks had to be inserted between the capstan bar and the lid so that the pressure could be maintained on what was a constantly diminishing amount of liquid. What came out from these repeated pressings was what was known as *strizzo*, literally squeezed or wrung out, which made a wine full of tannin but of inferior quality. Sometimes, if there was enough free-run wine to absorb it, some of the first of the *strizzo* was added to it. When we finished with the red we did the same thing to the white. It was then put into demijohns.

In a few weeks' time, while the wine was still fermenting, it would have to be racked off into other demijohns and the sediment removed; and during the winter months this would have to be done again.

What remained in the press after the *strizzo* had been extracted was a circular compressed mass of stalks and skin and pips that looked like a big fruit cake which Signor Giuseppe then extracted from the press by cutting it in half with an axe. These remains he used to make *grappa*, what the French call *marc*, in a still which he, as did many others, kept somewhere on his property, or else he spread it on our *vigneto* as a fertilizer.

In November, the long vine shoots would have to be cut off and collected for fuel and the vineyard manured and ploughed and the soil moved over the bases of the vines to protect them from the frost, and then the whole business began again. And when Signor Giuseppe took over the working of our *vigneto*, which he eventually did, the responsibility for finding the manure, which was already becoming as expensive as gold dust, that is if you could find it, devolved on me.

The result of all this often frenetic activity was that we had altogether succeeded in producing about 300 litres of wine, what was, with the threatened demise of some of the older vines, a totally inadequate quantity to meet our needs, and those of any future visitors. It was obvious that if we were going to increase our production we would have to buy more grapes and plant more vines. The sooner the better as it would be at least three years before any newly planted vines produced any grapes.

A week after our mini-*vendemmia* took place the Dadà asked us if we would like to help them with their *vendemmia*. The invitation was conveyed by Rina to Wanda when she went up the hill to collect the milk. At that time neither of us realized that being asked to help was a compliment because it meant that we were regarded as being potentially hard workers and would therefore earn the prodigious amounts of wine and food that would be served up to us in the course of the *vendemmia*.

Meanwhile, in order to stave off what looked like being a vineless/wineless future if nothing was done about it, I started work on enlarging the vineyard.

Under the auspices of Signor Giuseppe and with the help of Attilio, I began to excavate three trenches, each about seventy feet long, four feet deep and four feet wide, on one of the terraces below the house that had not been planted with vines for many years. It had to be a minimum of four or five years before the land was used again for this purpose.

The sub-soil was heavy clay with large stones embedded in it. The same sort of awful terrain that I had encountered when I had been digging out the septic tank.

When it came to digging, Attilio was a worker of what could only be described as frenetic energy. Wielding a pick, with a handle that was almost as tall as he was, and a spade, with a handle nearly twice his height, he hurled up great clods from the depths of the trench, like an actor in an old Keystone Cops film in which everything is accelerated, all the while talking away to himself nineteen to the dozen. Seeing him thus, going full blast, it was obvious why he was so much in demand when it came to doing *giornate*.

To keep us going, Wanda took time off from the seemingly

endless task of priming and undercoating and painting the window frames and shutters, and doing the laundry without a *vasca*, to bring us food and drink.

The weather was beautiful, too beautiful, one golden glaring day following another, but the evenings were already autumnal and we burned olive logs to keep ourselves warm. Signor Giuseppe had been wrong to start his *vendemmia* so early.

It was a gargantuan task we were involved in, possibly one of the last vineyards to be dug in the area using only picks and spades. The next time we wanted to enlarge it still more in a year or two's time the whole thing was done in a few hours with a bulldozer, and this included levelling the hillside behind the house as well as trenching it. Altogether it took us about five days and it was the hardest digging I had engaged in since 1940 when the Infantry Division of which I was a member was given the task of digging a trench system across Kent when the invasion of Britain appeared to be imminent.

'Heh!' Attilio said, when we had finally finished, as a sort of warning shot across my bows to announce that he was going to say something further. By this time I was a clay-stained wreck, sodden with perspiration, he immaculate in his cotton jacket and trousers, white shirt and cap – admittedly he had some clay on the toe caps of his boots. '*Heh! Adesso dobbiamo buttare un po' di concime nel buco,*' he said. 'Now we must throw some manure in the hole.'

'And what do we do then, Attilio?' I asked him.

'*Poi dobbiamo riempirlo di terra,*' he said, chuckling away. 'Then we fill it in.' And this was what we did, having thrown in some manure and rotting vegetation, solemnly filled them in, something we had never had to do after digging trenches in Kent. All this to give the roots of the vines a chance to establish themselves in this heavy-as-lead soil.

Altogether we planted five different sorts of vines, both red and white, which everyone said was a help against disease. We made the holes about three feet apart, in which we planted rooted vines which we got from a nursery down in the plain near Sarzana.

Just before planting them Attilio put in a little sand as a further encouragement. Altogether there weren't all that many but, by some miracle, only two failed to take.

At half past six the following morning, the day after Attilio and I finally completed our excavations and the subsequent infilling of the trenches at I Castagni, Wanda and I presented ourselves at the kitchen door of the Dadà establishment, dressed in our most rustic and ruined clothing – a *vendemmia* is hard on clothes, as we had discovered when doing our own. Each of us was armed with a pair of ordinary domestic scissors and a knife, which was all we could muster at the time – we had no secateurs. Apart from Rina and Signora Maria, there was no one else in sight, although various banging sounds and the deep rumbling of male voices from the direction of the cellar suggested that something of an important nature was going on there.

Rina had just finished the milking and she gave us some coffee, with *grappa*, which at this time in the morning was like a shot in the arm.

Up here the sun had not yet reached the plateau on which the house stood and was still hidden from view behind the big buttresses in the Apuan Alps, and everything was still in cold shadow and our breath smoked. Tranquillo's tractor was already waiting outside in the yard, hitched to the big trailer which had a power drive to its axle from the tractor. This was the one he used when hauling timber out of the woods.

Gradually, almost imperceptibly, the yard began to fill with people, some of whom we had never seen before, Signor Modesto and Tranquillo, who had been banging bungs into barrels in the cellar; Tranquillo's brother, pale, quiet Valentino, who didn't look like a countryman at all, who would be in charge of the grape crusher; Rina's sister, the one who was married to the local postman; the sister who lived next to the Dadà, and her husband; and their father, elderly, erect, with a fine, grey moustache, whose first name we never learned in all the years we knew him. And others too, whom neither of us can now remember. No one spoke very much. It was too early for conversation.

Now we began to load the trailer with everything that would be needed during the day: the *bigonci*, a lot of light wooden boxes picked up in the fruit market at Sarzana, useful for carrying the grapes to the sorting tables; and a lot of shallow wicker baskets with iron hooks on them, several triangular ladders and a couple of folding tables.

Now the sun came shooting up from behind the high peaks above Carrara, flooding the plateau on which Casa Dadà stood with a brilliant golden light, so that it seemed that everything around us was swimming in melted butter.

And now Tranquillo, as if to announce the coming of the sun, which needed no announcement, started up his tractor which roared into life with a great exploding sound. And those of us who were destined to take part in the picking of the grapes followed him on foot as he drove down to the main road. There he made a sharp left turn on to it and then a right turn off it down a rough, steep track past Signor Giuseppe's new house into what was Dadà territory, with the three men in the trailer who were going to be in charge of the *bigonci* holding on for dear life.

It was a beautiful prospect that opened up before us as we went down the hill. There was not a breath of wind and the smoke from the cooking fires rose in tall slim columns straight into the air from the farmsteads that dotted the hillside, some of them with a solitary cypress growing close to them. Immediately below us, in the direction in which we were bound, the hill fell away in a funnel-shaped valley, the lower end of which was still in deep shadow, dark and mysterious. Above it on a ridge, overlooking the Plain and the city of Sarzana, was the great, grim, geometrical Fortezza di Sarzanello built by Castruccio Castracani, in 1322, three years before he became master of Pisa and Tuscany and the scourge of the Florentines. Somewhere down there, reached by a series of tracks which were either ancient rights of way or else were used by mutual agreement between the various owners of the land, were other Dadà properties, not only the property of Signor Modesto but of people who belonged to other distant ramifications of the family.

There was only one road in the entire valley, a narrow, winding lane that wound its way round the head of it and gradually descended, eventually ending up in Sarzana. This was the route Attilio always followed when he went down to it from I Castagni.

Now, having crossed this road we entered a dream-like landscape, travelling down long, green tunnels of vines with steep banks wet with dew to one side and roofed in by *pergole* in which the trellises that supported the vines seemed to be groaning under the weight of the bunches of grapes; a landscape in which every seemingly endless vista led to another, as in a dream. And we passed through vineyards which were only a few years old, in contrast to those in the *pergole*, some of which had been planted half a century or more ago. These new *vigneti* were all planted in accordance with modern practice in long, wide spaced, parallel rows, supported by horizontal wires and canes one above the other, held up at each end of a row by baulks of timber which were anchored in the ground to boulders. They allowed much more sunlight to warm the grapes than the *pergole*.

The first of Signor Modesto's fields that we came to, the ones furthest from the house, a long way down the hill, where the shadows were just dispersing, consisted of half a dozen steep banks one above the other, each one about eight feet high and overhung with vines, those on the downhill side supported on wooden poles.

Here a number of *bigonci* were unloaded, the tables and ladders were set up and we were each given a basket with an iron hook on it, although some people had brought their own. By this time there were about twenty people in the field, some of whom would be cutting the grapes, others carrying them to the sorting tables and there were the heroes whose job it was, among other tasks, to lift the *bigonci* when they were full and hoist them on to the trailer.

These *pergole*, although extremely picturesque, were difficult to work in because in them the grapes had a remarkable capacity for concealing themselves among the leaves high overhead. The best way to harvest them was to sit on top of the bank with one's legs dangling down over it, getting nice and wet from the dew in the process, and grope for the bunches among the leaves. Then, when you had cut as many as possible, the next step was to erect one of the three-legged ladders under the *pergole* and gather the bunches from below; but sometimes the ground was so uneven that the ladder keeled over and on one occasion left me dangling in mid-air from one of the supporting wires, rather like a male gorilla swinging about in the treetops.

Among the worst things you could do was to upset your basket when it was full of grapes and hooked on to one of the supporting wires of a *pergola*, scattering them over a wide area in the grass below, from which they had to be retrieved, each and every one of them. To lose grapes that you had harvested in this way was unacceptable, although no one ever said so. You could tell it was unacceptable by the care with which anyone who happened to drop even two or three continued to look for them until they succeeded in finding them. You could eat as many grapes as you liked, though most people got bored with eating them; but losing them was another matter. The last thing you did when working on a section of any particular *pergola* was to slack off the pole which supported its outer edge which enabled you to reach the bunches that would have otherwise been out of reach.

From time to time some ancient trusty, whose active life swinging about under the *pergole* had more or less come to an end, would appear, take your basket, give you an empty one and pour the contents of your own into one of the boxes from the fruit market. If you had a basket you were particularly fond of and wanted to go on using it, you put the grapes in the box yourself and, if it was full, carried it to the sorting tables.

The best instruments for cutting the grapes were secateurs; scissors didn't exert enough pressure and were hopeless if, as I am, you are left-handed; knives were good but it was quite easy to cut off one of your own fingers on your other hand instead of a bunch of grapes, or even someone else's finger if they were working on the other side of the vine, although I never heard of such a thing happening. By the end of the first day both Wanda and I had succeeded in cutting our own fingers and after this we used secateurs. Some hardy characters broke off the bunches with their bare hands without losing any grapes, always a source of wonderment to me.

At the tables hawk-eyed ladies subjected our offerings to further scrutiny and cleansing. Here too, the number of stalks was further reduced by pruning. Sometimes if a bunch obviously had nothing wrong with it they filleted it by taking it in one hand and then stripping the grapes from it with the other, straight into a *bigoncio*. If any bunches were affected by mildew, they were got rid of at this time.

Some bunches, especially good ones, were ear-marked for eating later in the year and, when possible, these had their stems cut into a T-shape so that they could be hung on nails on a wall of the cellar until they were needed.

Other bunches we were told to leave on the vines so that they could continue to ripen until the onset of the *Estate di San Martino*, St Martin's Summer, otherwise Martinmas, 11 November. You had to be very careful not to cut any of these grapes by mistake which was horribly easy to do. I did it once, buried the evidence, and went to work in another part of the *vigneto* as far from the scene of the crime as possible. The loss was noted but I was not suspected, at least I didn't think so.

These were fine grapes from old *pergole*, like those at I Castagni, anything from thirty to forty years old, or even more. Black and white grapes with a beautiful velvety bloom on them and oozing juice. Looking at them, it was difficult to believe that these skins, so good to look at, housed millions of microscopic moulds, bacteria and yeasts which between them performed the fermentation process for the making of wine.

When there were more filled *bigonci* than empty ones, or at some moment which Tranquillo or his father deemed to be the *momento giusto*, they were hoisted on to the trailer, which stood a good five feet above the ground, by those chosen for this particular form of torment and then Tranquillo would haul them and the *bigonci* up the hill to the cellar for the crushing operation.

It was important to keep the supply of *bigonci* turning over. One of the worst things that can happen at a *vendemmia* when it is going full blast, apart from a leak developing in the bottom of some enormous barrel, or a hailstorm developing, is for whoever is in charge of the proceedings to discover that all the *bigonci* are full. When this happens and the baskets are also full and the boxes are full and the sorting tables are groaning under the weight of grapes that can no longer be sorted because there are no *bigonci*, the system grinds to a halt. But in a well-run *vendemmia* such a mishap is unlikely to occur unless the tractor or the grape crusher, or both of them at the same time, give up the ghost. The trouble with grapes in a *vendemmia* is that in some way they bear a resemblance to sewage, which still goes on arriving at the sewage outfall even if orders are given that no more can be accepted for the time being because the place is awash with it.

By about ten o'clock, after having worked for about three hours among the *pergole* in this lowest field and having stripped them of grapes, everyone was beginning to feel like a rest, and a drink. 'Another three hours like this,' Wanda said, 'and I'm going to feel a bit done-in.' It was therefore a very welcome surprise for us when Rina and her two sisters appeared on the scene, each with a hamper perched on her head with a piece of rolled up cloth underneath it to take the weight; all three of them very erect – you can scarcely be anything else with a heavy weight balanced on your noddle. In fact they looked like the sort of women who walk interminably round Etruscan pots. The baskets contained a *merenda* for some twenty persons, for that was what we amounted to, something everyone except ourselves had been anticipating, but for us a welcome surprise, and they now proceeded to set it out on a large white tablecloth which they spread on the grass.

The place chosen was shaded from the heat of the sun by a plantation of canes and by trees and lush vegetation. And there was a spring which, if you removed a wooden plug from it, discharged a jet of water into a sort of miniature aqueduct made with the trunks of small trees which had been split in half and hollowed out and joined to the next one, which conveyed the water to some other part of the property.

Here and there long shafts of sunlight penetrated the dark shadows cast by the vegetation overhead, and when an occasional ripple of wind passed through this glade everything was dappled with light and shade. It was a magical place and one to which we always looked forward to returning.

It was a memorable *merenda*. Almost everything was home-made and of the best. There was *pecorino* cheese brought down by a shepherd whose flock was in the high pastures beyond a place called Campo Cecina; there was the same sort of *mortadella* we had eaten at lunch on Easter Sunday; and there was *coppa*, a *salame* made from pig's head, the neck, muscles and rind, which comes from around Parma. And there were great loaves of bread baked in the Dadà oven, and lots of last year's wine, red and white, and glasses to drink it from, and sharp knives to cut the bread, which some people did, sawing towards their chests or bosoms in what appeared to be a highly dangerous fashion.

As always at a picnic there was a certain amount of holding back among those invited to take part, but not all that much, and very soon everyone was tucking in and talking away while the bottles began to circulate.

The conversation was difficult to follow as it was conducted for the most part in dialect and the speakers had their mouths stuffed with gobbets of *pane nostrano*, *mortadella*, *formaggio* and *coppa*, just as ours were, or else were knocking back the *vino*, just as we were too.

To some extent the talk concerned itself with ancient rights and wrongs, particularly differences of opinion about boundaries and rights of way which one could see, only by looking at the terrain, would be about as safe to get involved in as entering a minefield, as we would one day discover for ourselves.

But much more popular as a subject of conversation with everyone were the current scandals – about what happened when her doctor had sent Signora A. off from Sarzana to Montecatini Terme for a fortnight's spa treatment for arthritis and she had returned home after completing the course with her arthritis cured, but *incinta*, in the family way. All because a newly hired masseur got lost on the way to give a male customer the treatment and had ended up in a cubicle with the Signora in the ladies' wing.

And how a similar fate, if that is how it could be described, had recently befallen a priest's housekeeper at the ripe old age of forty-one, who had presented Don Whatever-His-Name-Was with a living and breathing male ex-voto. '*Un miracolo*' was how the mother had described it. '*Un'ospite inatteso*' was how one of the female grape pickers described the infant, 'An unexpected guest'.

And about Signor C. and his wife who had a modest but thriving *bar/ristorante* on the Via Aurelia that had recently been closed after a raid by the police because it was alleged that it was also being used as a *bordello*. And why no further action was going to be taken in the matter because Signor C.'s wife, who also did the accounts for her husband's *bar/ristorante/bordello*, was the daughter of a police inspector, which was why Signor C. got away with a not very large fine, for using his premises as a twelve-bedroomed hotel when it was only licensed as a *bar/ristorante*. The following year, Signor and Signora C.'s enterprise found itself included in a list of recommended hotels.

And about how a postman from a place in the valley of the Magra had found himself running into danger when he delivered a registered letter to a lady from her husband who was supposed to be far away in a tanker in the Persian Gulf; but walked in just as the Signora, who was of an ample size, had invited the postman in for a quick glass of wine while she signed for it.

'For a "*brindisi*", a toast to my husband's safe return,' was how she described it.

'He would have needed one of these *tramalli* to get on top of her, that *postino* would,' someone said.

'It's not true that he would need a ladder,' one man said. 'He's got such a big *cazzo* that he could have done it lying on his back on the floor, and she could have been on the bed.'

'How do you know,' several people asked, 'about his *cazzo* being so big?'

'I was at school with him, I saw it when I was in *scuola media*. He showed it to me in the *gabinetto*. He was very proud of it. Anyone could have a look, but if you weren't a friend you had to give him a sweet.'

'Would he let you touch it?' an elderly lady, who looked a pillar of propriety, asked.

'Yes,' he said, 'but you had to give him a lot of sweets and I never had enough. Besides, I was never a close friend.'

The only boring conversations were the ones directed at the two of us by people we had never met before. How many children had we got? Only two! And why was the weather so *brutta* in *Inghilterra*? And were we friendly with *la Regina* and if so did we see her often; and did we like *l'Italia* – 'Bella l'Italia, non è vero?' And did we have wine in *Inghilterra* and *caccia*, and what was the food like, and were either of us *Protestanti*? (Great relief when Wanda announced that she wasn't; a lot of sympathy for me – frequent use of the word *poveretto!* – for having been born one.) And what did we think of Pope Paul VI? Whereas all we wanted was to hear more about the lady whose husband was supposed to be on a tanker in the Persian Gulf, or whatever it was that was under discussion at that particular moment.

It was a happy scene; the women and girls with their short skirts and aprons and their head scarves – the big straw hats they wore in the open fields when the sun was high were no good under the *pergole* as they kept on getting knocked off by the branches overhead. With their scarves on they looked like participants in an Italian version of *The Pirates of Penzance*.

And the men were in their oldest but not dirtiest clothes, the more elderly wearing corduroy trousers and waistcoats, the younger ones in jeans; clothes that had been cobbled together with infinite patience by wives and mothers and grandmothers with the leftovers from other clothes, so that some of them looked like patchwork quilts.

Then, after we had finished eating, we lay on our backs for a few minutes, looking up at the sky through the now autumnal leaves, listening to the drone of the insects, not all of them of a friendly disposition; listening to the now diminishing conversation which had become a drone also, carried on now by only the most determined gas-bags. There was not the sight or sound of a bird. To anyone coming here from England their absence from the countryside was uncanny. The following year a nightingale settled in the wood above I Castagni, thrilled us with its song for a while, then departed, came back the next year and the next, and then was never heard or seen again.

But it was not for more than a couple of minutes, this business of lying on one's back, in my case still thinking about the postman, and gazing at the sky. Then we were on our feet picking up our various cutting implements and our baskets; Rina and the other two girls were packing up the remains of the *merenda*; Tranquillo was starting up the tractor; and we all set off together up the hill to the next *vigneto*, this one of the more modern, open-cast sort, exposing the grapes, mostly red Trebbiano and red Sangiovese and red and white Malvasia and white Vermentino, to the full heat of the sun, and the pickers, both male and female, also.

As we stripped vine after vine rather like locusts, we began to identify things that we would remember the next year and in the following years; but this first *vendemmia* was a journey of discovery: a hollow tree with vines and wild roses climbing up it, only the roses reachable, even with a ladder, the grapes blooming mockingly overhead; a secretive-looking barn without a single window in it; a grass-grown crater made by one of the enormous projectiles fired from the gun on Isola Palmaria in 1945.

As we advanced uphill from one *vigneto* to another with what seemed infinite slowness, rather like a band of beaters at a shoot, more and more enfilades of *pergole* opened up ahead of us on either hand, stretching away into the distance, new worlds that up to now we had not known existed. It was like a voyage of discovery through some uncharted, arcadian archipelago in a tropical sea.

There was no doubt about it being tropical. The sun resembled a huge gold medal suspended by an invisible ribbon high overhead in a sky that appeared to be incandescent, and the wind that had caressed us while we were eating the *merenda* now two long hours ago had died away. Everyone was sticky and stained with grape juice, and thirsty, but the wine in the wine bottles left over from the *merenda* was by now too warm to satisfy anyone's thirst, though some of the men, including myself, still had an occasional swig at it. Any water available was lukewarm. Everyone was longing for a wash, a cool drink and a chance to sit down and eat the promised midday meal, about which the two of us knew nothing. We thought the *merenda* was lunch.

In fact it was long after midday, about a quarter to one, before we reached the main road by Signor Giuseppe's house from which we had set out originally, and went up into the Dadà farmyard.

There, the last of the morning's gathering of grapes was being fed into the grape crusher, a job which, even more than I had appreciated earlier on, I now recognized as being one I had up to now been incredibly fortunate to avoid being involved in.

Then the clattering noise made by the crusher suddenly ceased and there was nothing but the rumble of voices of the people in the yard. But these were almost immediately obliterated by a succession of ear-splitting noises emitted by the klaxon of the local bus as its driver, a young man with ginger hair, took it up through the bends from Caniparola to Fosdinovo, depositing two other Dadà kinswomen armed and dressed for the *vendemmia* at the bus stop, 'Just in time for the lunch', as one of the men who had been emptying *bigonci* into the grape crusher all the morning rather unkindly put it.

A tap in the farmyard fed a deep, oblong marble trough the size and shape of a sarcophagus which, until recently, had been used to store olive oil, a receptacle much in use for this purpose in these parts where marble was commonplace; and there we queued up for a wash after taking a long cool drink from the tap.

Because it was such a hot day, instead of eating indoors as we would normally have done, two long trestle tables had been set up end to end in the open air under a very old *pergola*. Heavy with black grapes which, sometime the following day, we would be picking, it gave shade to the whole of the southern side of the house. Down below the valley was lost in haze. The freezing wind and rain that had buffeted us on our way through the streets of Fosdinovo in the procession on Good Friday and the similar conditions that had prevailed even longer ago when we had acquired I Castagni now seemed not just a few months ago but a whole age away. It was difficult to believe that those days had ever happened, just as it was difficult to believe that we had eaten a *merenda* only about two and a half hours previously. Now all we could think of was lunch.

We each sat where we could find a place. There was no established order. No drinks were offered before the meal, just as they weren't at anyone else's *vendemmia*, apart from the wine we had drunk at the *merenda* and the occasional swigs we had taken from the bottles down in the fields during the morning. And now, when they did begin drinking, most people drank either red or white, rarely both. To drink both at the same meal was thought to be injurious to health, '*Fa male allo stomaco*,' they all said.

For lunch we were given *brodo*, a clear soup made from beef and chicken stock, followed by *manzo bollito*, boiled beef, stuffed with a mixture of spinach, egg, *grana*, and then *mortadella*, the real *mortadella* from Bologna, the pink sort with peppercorns and squares of white fat and goodness knows what else in it, a sort of sausage I never really liked, although Wanda was crazy about it.

After this there was *pollo arrosto* and *pollo bollito*, roasted and boiled chicken that had been chopped up with a murderous looking chopper and the bones broken. The chickens killed for these dishes were the sort that up to now had spent their entire lives scratching a living in the Dadà farmyard, the same sort we had already eaten on Easter Sunday.

And there were more of the wonderful potatoes we had also eaten on Easter Sunday, and the bitter green salad called *radicchio* eaten with oil and vinegar, and plates of tomatoes to be eaten with oil, salt and pepper but without vinegar which would make them too acid, and as much wine as anyone felt like drinking. Then there was coffee, but no *grappa* or cognac, and no five minutes rest afterwards, either. These were reserved for the evening. By now it was conceded, even by Tranquillo, who usually took a rather pessimistic view of anything growing, that this was going to be a good year for wine.

✢

'*Vorrei chiederle un piacere*' ('I want to ask you a favour') said a deep voice from behind me which I recognized immediately as being Tranquillo's. I knew what was coming next: '*un po' di aiuto coi le bigonci*' ('a bit of help with the *bigonci*').

He was wearing the peaked cotton cap with the maker's name on it with which the agents for the tractor had graciously presented him when he bought it. It was an early version of one of those long-peaked platypus caps that US presidents wear when trundling around golf courses in little electrically propelled carts instead of walking and then wonder why they have blood pressure problems.

I was trapped. I should have taken refuge in the lavatory, the one that at that time was in the open air, hidden, as ours was at I Castagni, in the midst of a plantation of *canne*, and only emerged when Tranquillo had found someone else to do the job. Perhaps I could even have offered to do the washing up – there were no washing-up machines, even ten years later – which would effectively have queered me with the whole Dadà clan. They would have thought I was the sort of *Inglese* who wears a ballet skirt in the privacy of his home. Men simply did not wash up in any part of Italy I had ever visited, and many of them still don't, except in television commercials.

It was not that I objected to carrying heavy weights – anything in a rucksack or a pack or lashed to a pack frame was fine. What I didn't like carrying were weights not really adapted to being carried, such as sacks filled to the brim with Australian grain, as I had had to when I was a sailor in 1939, or, what was worse, carrying a sack of rice across a ridge of the Apennines in the winter of 1943, which almost finished me off, or in 1941, helping to carry the corpse of an enormous member of the Indian civil service to a cemetery beside the Ganges when the temperature was up in the hundreds.

However, I could scarcely fail him, especially after eating such an enormous, delicious lunch.

'*Lei, soffre d'ernia?*' he asked. It seemed a bit late in the day for him to ask if I suffered from hernia.

'Not up to now,' I said.

✣

There were three of us who were going to be involved with the *bigonci*, and the crushing of the grapes, now that the other lot had been stood down, four with Tranquillo. One was a deceptively fragile-looking man of about sixty; the other was a boy of about twenty, a Dadà nephew, bursting with energy, who looked like an advertisement for Shredded Wheat.

Looking at them I wondered if they had been subjected to some kind of medical examination before being pronounced free of hernias. If so, why hadn't I been given one? Why hadn't I simply said that I had a hernia? No one could prove it either way without undressing me. The questions came crowding in.

I soon discovered that when we weren't slinging *bigonci* around, or feeding grapes into the crusher up at the house, or those already crushed into various barrels, we were expected to carry on cutting grapes down in the *vigneti* and putting them into the baskets and the boxes and transporting them to the sorting tables. We did this until such time as Tranquillo, who was also doing all these things except lifting *bigonci*, gave the order to begin the loading operations.

The *bigonci* were slightly oval in shape and were made in the same way as a barrel, using staves. Just like the barrels, they too had to be thoroughly soaked in water for at least a couple of days before the *vendemmia* began, but unlike barrels they could be made to nest one inside the other when empty. Because of this they had no handles, which made them slippery things to deal with when fully loaded. In fact, all in all, they were not very well adapted for the purpose for which they were constructed, as empty they weighed about as much as their contents; but there was no doubt they were picturesque.

Soon these wooden *bigonci* would begin to be superseded by plastic ones which were much lighter and didn't have to be soaked in water before they were used, as they were pressed in a mould, just as the straw covers that had been used to cover the wine *fiaschi* since time immemorial were being replaced by plastic ones. Nevertheless, it says something for the innate conservatism of most *contadini* that wooden *bigonci* still continue to be used in many parts of Italy to this day.

By the time we reached the next *vigneto*, having loaded the empty *bigonci* on to the trailer up at the house, those who had set off before us had already got quite a lot of bunches on to the sorting tables, and as soon as we got there we dumped a number of *bigonci* as close to the tables as we could, before picking up the secateurs and setting off with our baskets to start cutting.

As soon as we had done this the women working at the tables began to fill the first of these *bigonci* with grapes, while one of the men, to make room for more, squashed them down into them using a piece of wood for the purpose.

By the time we got to the end of this particular *vigneto*, a large number of *bigonci* had already been filled and were ready to be taken back to the cellar.

The first thing was to get the *bigoncio* up on to one of my shoulders, which in my case was insufficiently covered in flesh to support it in anything but acute discomfort, in one hoist from the ground. This was the first of three or four moments in which the possibility of getting a hernia seemed to me to be really quite high. Well, it felt quite high. The next was when you walked with the *bigoncio* to the place where Tranquillo had parked his tractor and the trailer. Sometimes, if you were lucky, there would be Tranquillo or Signor Modesto or another member of the *bigoncio* party to help you transfer it from your shoulder up on to the floor of the trailer.

Then, when the *bigonci* were all loaded, Tranquillo started up the engine and we all three, the fragile-looking man, the boy who looked as if he lived on Shredded Wheat and myself, scrambled aboard and set off, thrown from side to side of the trailer, on the rough ride to the cellar. As soon as we reached it, the sides of the trailer were lowered and Valentino switched on the current and either the so-called fragile man or the young one poured the contents of a *bigoncio* into the jaws of the crusher which squashed them and then let them fall into another *bigoncio* which was set up underneath it. When it was full Valentino switched off the current. The third man, who I couldn't help noticing always happened to be me, lifted the loaded *bigoncio* which contained the crushed grapes on to his shoulder with the aid of one of the others, first replacing it with an empty one, and then tottered up a rather unstable wooden ramp to where, overhead, the barrels were set up, and poured the contents into one or other of them, depending on whether they were black or white grapes. What the punishment was for getting mixed up and pouring black grapes into a barrel with white ones already in it was unimaginable.

The afternoon seemed longer and harder and even hotter than the morning had been because most of the *vigneti* were planted in the modern way and, as a result, the terrain was much less shaded. And there was no five o'clock tea break, as there used to be in England before the war at harvest time, although wine was still available.

Sometimes we found ourselves toiling up long lines of vines and down again in the next parallel row at an angle of about fifty degrees. At least here, unlike working in the *pergole*, you could see and talk to your neighbours or the persons working on the other side of the vines.

Often the conversation became lubricious. It was usually the most strait-laced-looking elderly characters, like the old lady who had been so interested in the postman's equipment, who had the most hair-raising repertoires, but those at the Dadà *vendemmie* were mild compared with what was on offer at some others. Some of them sounded like excerpts from some hitherto unpublished work, *The Sexual Life of the Contadini*, with chapters such as 'Fun in the Loft'. But mostly it was all good, straight, missionary position stuff: no incest, no bestiality. It was nice to be in a place where even the animals felt safe.

We worked on until the sun went down as a blood-red orb behind the Cinque Terre, the coastal area beyond La Spezia where those who were engaged in the *vendemmie* were doing the most difficult work of all.

Difficult, because their *vigneti* were so steep to the sea and the vines grew so low that they required the expenditure of an enormous amount of energy to harvest them. There, at that time, it was quite common to see men and women carrying *bigonci* on their shoulders for long distances from the *vigneto* to the nearest road. This wine of the Cinque Terre was, if genuine, almost impossible to find in commerce.

Another few days and it would already be dark when Italian wintertime, which began earlier than it does in Britain, came into force; but now it was still only dark around seven. That day we had succeeded in clearing all the Dadà grapes from the valley west of the road. The following day we would clear the ridge on which their farmhouse was situated, all the way up from the seventeenth bend where the shops and the Communist cell were. That was if it didn't rain; but not even the most pessimistic amateur meteorologists, even Signor Giuseppe, could really prophesy that.

Back at the cellar, another half-hour was to pass before we had finished emptying the last of the *bigonci* into the barrels, and when we had done so Tranquillo dished out drinks to his hernia-less helpers, and no one said anything about the dangers of drinking on an empty stomach.

I was done-in, and so was almost everyone else, including Wanda. Suddenly we felt very cold.

Dinner was not for another half-hour. There was just time to slip down the hill to I Castagni and have a shower under our wonderful Velodoccia, the replacement model for the one Signor Bergamaschi, the plumber, had blown a hole in, change our clothes and get up the hill again for dinner.

Now we all sat down again, this time in the kitchen, with Rina's son Paolo, who would be taking part in the *vendemmia* the following day because it was a Saturday and there was no school. We ate homemade *ravioli*; then more meat and chicken – for some reason there was never pork. Usually there would also have been a dish of *funghi in umido*, but the hot, dry weather that was so good for the grapes was no good for *funghi*. And there was a lot of wine drunk, red and white. Then there was cheese and lots of walnuts, with which we drank some of Signor Modesto's stronger, sweeter wines, and coffee.

Chapter Fourteen

THE FOLLOWING DAY proved to be a boiling hot twin of the previous one; and as we climbed rather stiffly up the hill to report for duty at the Casa Dadà, we heard excited cries of 'Signora! Signora!' from the field below the track, at the point where I had contrived to get one of the hubs of the Land Rover stuck on the tree.

Thinking that something was seriously amiss we looked over the edge down to where a magnificent, jolly-looking, black-eyed, black-haired girl was rinsing sheets in the *vasca*. (Later, Signor Giuseppe built us one too, and I dug a long trench to connect it with a spring.) She introduced herself as Signora Franca, the wife of Dadà Nino, son of a Signor Dadà Armando who was a member of a collateral family of Dadà. They had only been married comparatively recently and from this time onward we both knew her as 'The Young Bride'.

She was the bearer of a message to us from Signor Armando.

'They have sent me,' she said, 'to ask you if you would like to come and assist at their *vendemmia*. It is beginning tomorrow morning and will only last a couple of days.'

'I don't know what you think,' I said in English to Wanda, who had already admitted to suffering from various aches and pains in parts of her anatomy which had been completely pain-free up to now. I myself was surprisingly well, apart from my right shoulder blade which felt as if it had been hit with a sledge hammer. 'I think we should have a day off. It isn't only the *bigonci*. It's all the food and drink.'

'Don't tell me,' Wanda said, 'that you're worried about being given too much drink. I simply don't believe it. I know it's hard, the work with the *bigonci*, but they are doing us an honour by inviting us.'

'It's also something to do with me not having a hernia,' I said.

'Anyway,' she went on, 'I think we should say "yes" we would like to do their *vendemmia*,' and before we could even discuss the subject a bit more she had done so. I was quite glad really, apart from the *bigonci*.

Up at the Dadà house we again borrowed a couple of pairs of secateurs and set off for the final assault on the Dadà *vigneti* which were disposed in large numbers across a gently sloping plateau.

There were no steep bits but there were still lots of *pergole* situated in places that were difficult to get at: over ditches with water in them; around the walls of barns, and around the shed in which Rina kept her cow. It was a Saturday, and lots of children were in the fields with their parents, the larger ones sliding down the banks of the *pergole*, sometimes hurting themselves a bit, the smaller ones getting lost when about ten feet from their mothers and rushing off in search of them in the wrong direction, mooing.

In spite of having done what I considered to be my stint with the *bigonci*, I still found myself a member of the party dealing with them; but this time I only had to hoist them on to the trailer and when I did this I made sure that someone else, such as the Shredded Wheat boy, gave me a hand. The rather fragile, elderly man who had been part of the team the previous day got the job of pouring the grapes into the crusher and then the squashed ones into the barrels, but he seemed completely indestructible. This time the *merenda* took place, as did lunch, back at the house, in the shade of the big pergola.

That evening, when it was almost dark, the last grapes of the Dadà *vendemmia* were harvested from this same pergola. And then there was dinner, with, just as the lunch had been, a completely different series of dishes from those we had eaten the previous day. What Rina and Signora Maria had accomplished was a remarkable feat but no one said, '*Brave le cuoche!*' ('well done, the cooks!'). And that was it for another year.

Everything was as safely stowed as it could be in the cellar, unless a hurricane took the roof off. Like everyone else the Dadà could only hope for a successful outcome to their labours; but in the event there was no cause for alarm. It was a good year for everyone, even the Newbys with their mini-*vendemmia*.

This other Dadà family lived in a tall, old, grey stone farm-house that had never been given the *sangue di bue* treatment. It was built over a cellar that, although cavernous, was above ground and it stood on a sort of headland, on which a grove of cypresses flourished. You got to it by continuing downhill on the track from Signora Angiolina's place without turning off to the right on the curve that led down to I Castagni. If you continued on down this track beyond this Dadà house you reached the back road which eventually led to Sarzana. This was the one which Attilio used to zoom down on foot on market days, refusing all offers of lifts – '*Ho già avuto una macchina*' ('I have already had a motor car'), was what we always expected him to say on these occasions, just as he used to say '*Ho già mangiato*' or '*Ho già bevuto*' ('I have already eaten' or 'I have already had a drink'), when offered any sustenance at unscheduled hours of day or night. The only real exception to this rule of his was when he was telling his stories, when he enjoyed a drink or two to keep him going.

Signor Dadà Armando was a strikingly handsome man. Whenever we met him, whether indoors or out, he always wore a very battered brown felt hat which he changed from a rather unre-markable piece of headgear, by an expert twist of the brim, into something very debonair, in rather the same way as Fred Astaire, when setting out for an encounter with Ginger Rogers, was able to give an inimitably elegant air to the wearing of a top hat, sim-ply by giving it a light tap.

It is probable that Signor Armando wore his hat all the time because he was bald; but we never found out whether this was so because he never raised it to us, or took it off in our presence. For all we knew he might quite well have worn it in bed. If Attilio went to bed with his umbrella up it was not difficult to imagine Signor Armando in bed with his hat on.

But this business of the hat was not the only resemblance Signor Armando bore to Fred Astaire, otherwise it wouldn't have been worth mentioning. It was because Signor Armando was renowned in the neighbourhood as a marvellous dancer in the way of *ballo liscio*, an expert in the waltz. In fact he was so adept that it was said that he could waltz on a table, providing he had a partner of sufficiently strong nerves. Subsequently we met many by then elderly ladies who, when asked about Signor Armando's capabilities as a dancer, still smiled dreamily when they recalled the blissful times they had spent in his arms, careering around the wooden dance floors under the trees, as Italy's answers to Ginger Rogers.

Signor Armando's wife was small and a great talker. It must have been a difficult role to sustain, keeping up with her husband in the particular role in which he had cast himself.

Their son, Nino, had spent his years of obligatory military service in the Customs Service, on various remote and what sounded like thoroughly unpleasant frontiers of Italy, before returning home to start a watch and clock repairing business in Sarzana. He really wanted to be a farmer, and would have been if his father had not suddenly decided to make a will in which he left the farmhouse and a large part of the land which went with it to a sister, who was not much interested in farming. At the same time Nino and his wife had to be content with a picturesque but uncomfortable barn across the yard which needed a lot of money spent on it to make it habitable and from which he had to commute by bus to Sarzana each day.

Armando's most distant *vigneti* were even further away down the valley than his namesake's. It took a long time to reach them. Some of his vines had stems that were the thickness of small trees. There was no real *merenda* on this first day of their *vendemmia*, but there was plenty of wine and very good bread which was cut up for us on site by Signora Franca. This absence of a *merenda* was not because of any meanness on the part of the *padrone* but simply because these distant *vigneti* were too far from the house to make it practicable for three women to carry a *merenda* down to them on their heads which, altogether, would take more than an hour there and back.

But lunch was memorable, served in a high-ceilinged, austere room, its walls lined with big, framed, black-and-white photographs of the family, dead and gone, which looked as if they had been processed in embalming fluid.

And that evening, while Franca cooked the evening meal, because it had grown cold again, a fire was lit in a fireplace that resembled a railway tunnel, a resemblance that was heightened by two parallel lengths of real railway line which protruded from it and acted as fire-irons; so that when the fire started discharging smoke into the room I half expected a miniature steam engine to come puffing out of it.

✝

However, of all the *vendemmie* we took part in during the following years the Bs' was the most memorable. They were never ready to start work however late the helpers turned up at their property, which was some way uphill from I Castagni. It was a big property from the point of view of wine production of which they were still *mezzadri*. With the Bs there was always some disaster either impending or happening. Either they had failed to invite sufficient people to help them do the job, which meant that their *vendemmia* went on for longer than it needed to, or they had asked them for the wrong day, or else had forgotten to ask anyone at all. Whatever it was they had omitted to do it always led to a lot of screaming from the open windows of their house to those of their potential helpers, which were dotted about the hillside, in the course of which the Bs attempted to rally their forces and get the show on the road.

'*GIUSEEPPE! DOVE SEEI?*' ('Where are you?') '*MARIIA! PERCHE NON SEI VENUUTA?*' ('Why haven't you come?')

Or sometimes they didn't allow enough time for the barrels and the *bigonci* to be soaked with water, and as a result the wooden staves hadn't swelled sufficiently, and there was nothing to put the *vendemmia* in. Or else the tractor broke down, or they forgot to ask the tractor driver to come. Or, most awful of all misfortunes which once befell them, when the bottom of one of their biggest barrels fell out of it and the entire contents were lost. Fortunately it was only a quarter full. The Bs were not only accident prone, they were lucky too.

Yet in spite of being almost impossible to work with they often made some of the best wine in the area. A lot of drink was drunk at the Bs' *vendemmia* when it finally got going. And the conversation was pretty wild.

If it rained during the *vendemmia*, and sometimes it did for long periods, it was hell. If it rained heavily the *vendemmia* had to stop because too much water got on to the grapes and into the *bigonci* and from them into the crusher and from that into the barrels with disastrous results.

When it rained a sack was the best thing to wear over the head and shoulders; wearing a waterproof coat in such conditions, long before the days of Gore-tex, was like being in a portable Turkish bath.

If the grapes were more or less a write-off, as they were in some years, and it rained heavily as well, it was indeed lugubrious. There was no *merenda*, one's boots got clogged up with great lumps of clay and if the rain did stop for a few minutes, enough time to fill a *bigonci*o or two, nothing could be done because the rain usually began to fall again, by which time the grapes were so wet that the whole business had to be abandoned for the rest of that day, and possibly the next and the next one, too.

The worst rain we ever experienced was during a *vendemmie* with the Cani family, who had a farm down the hill towards Caniparola beyond I Pilastri, the farm which had stone pillars to support the vines. This family was regarded locally as being almost as foreign as we were because they came from a place called Castelnovo ne' Monti on the other side of the Apennines in

Reggio nell' Emilia, where a vast rock looms over the town, the Pietra Bismantova. Signor Cani, the father, died not long after we got to know them and the two sons became expert tractor drivers who used to hire themselves out to the local farmers, and had the reputation of being very hard workers. Signora Cani, known as 'La Cani', was a wonderful, dynamic woman who used to sit on the roadside in season selling flowers and vegetables, as did many other ladies in the neighbourhood. She had a daughter named Alice, pronounced 'Aliche', a good-looking girl who remained unmarried although she had a number of admirers. She was a highly skilled dressmaker and made things for Wanda. It was a strange sensation sitting in her workroom leafing through *L'Officiel* and French *Vogue* in such a rural spot.

The first year we were invited by the Cani family to help with their *vendemmia*, it rained for three days and altogether took five days to complete. It was the *scirocco* from Africa that was to blame. Great forks of lightning hurled themselves down from the sky into the *vigneti*, as if trying to impale us where we crouched in terror under the *pergole*, too far from any human habitation for us to make a run for it, while the rain poured down and the thunder rolled. Soon we were forced to abandon the *pergole* when the rain came sweeping down over the steep banks in a series of coffee-coloured waterfalls and make for the Cani farmhouse, soaked to the skin, where a big fire had been kindled to dry us out. This *scirocco* caused a good deal of damage; but not half as much as it would have done if there had been hail, which could ruin all the grapes in a *vigneto* in a matter of minutes; but it never did in all the years we were at I Castagni.

Most lowering to the spirits were the years when there were so few grapes of good quality that people had to go further south in Tuscany, or to the market at Sarzana, to buy them.

It was never an enjoyable task buying grapes, partly because it almost always seemed to be raining when we engaged in it which was not surprising as it was rain and lack of sun that had caused the shortage in the first place. The grapes were in huge stacks of boxes all round the periphery of the market. The first time we went there to buy we enlisted the help of Signor Giuseppe whose very presence had the effect, to some extent, of keeping the prices down; but in fact they were more or less the same for everyone unless a very big deal was being done. At first it was not easy for Wanda and myself, sampling grapes from one of the boxes to know what they were – Sangiovese, Canaiolo, Trebbiano and so on, among reds; Vernaccia, Trebbiano and so on, among whites. Tasting these grapes, plucking up courage eventually to ask what sorts they were, for all we knew they could have come from Sicily or Molise.

At that time the market at Sarzana was near the railway station and was surrounded by shops selling seeds and agricultural instruments, and by little *caffès*. In spite of being in the town it had a genuinely rural air and every market day numbers of female *contadini*, including Signora Angiolina and Signora Fernanda and Signora Maria and Signora Cani, used to take up temporary residence inside the main hall where, sitting on upturned boxes, they offered for sale various sorts of home produce – cheese, eggs, fruit and vegetables.

Many years later the market was moved to an unattractive location on the outskirts of the town and it never again had the same feeling about it.

Another great *vendemmia* was that of our local postman (no relation to the other postman), who was married to one of Rina's sisters. The postman, a very jolly man, was one of the first people we got to know after we were finally installed at I Castagni. He used to bring us our mail, roaring down the bend to the house on a Vespa, later in a little Fiat. He often used to stop for a glass of wine which he drank while giving us all the latest information on what was going on.

When the last *vendemmia* had taken place, and the last dinner had been eaten, and the last wine drunk, we would all reel away under the stars, or through the rain to our various habitations, sometimes, if we had indulged too freely (a male defect in these parts at such times), falling into ditches which some thoughtless fellows seemed to have dug since we passed that way in the morning; and the next year would be the same with either more or less sun and better or worse grapes and wine, and so on *ad infinitum* – at the two Dadà *vendemmie*, the Canis', the Bs' (that is if they remembered to invite us), and at that of our postman. And sometimes there were others. This doing the *vendemmie* became an important part of our lives for more than twenty years to come.

Chapter Fifteen

ONE YEAR, after the various *vendemmie* had been brought to a successful conclusion, the weather broke and for the following three days the *scirocco* roared in from Africa by way of the Ligurian Sea and the rain fell in torrents, turning what had been almost iron-hard earth into a Passchendaele of mud. Then it stopped and the sun came out again but with less vigour than it had displayed previously. Now there was a distinctly autumnal feeling in the air. If I had been in England, I would have thought about eating crumpets and wearing a tweed coat.

Such conditions, rain after extreme heat, and then sun again, were right for what could be a spectacular growth of *funghi* within the next day or two.

These, if they did decide to appear, would probably be of the genus *boletus*, of which there are numerous sorts. The best are *boletus edulis* which have brown, shiny caps, known in Italy as *porcini*, in France as *cèpes*, in Germany as *Steinpilz* and in Britain, where until recently few people have ever heard of them let alone eaten them, as ceps or penny buns. Of the *boleti* only a couple of rare, highly coloured variants, *boletus satanas* and *boletus purpureus*, are poisonous but not usually fatally so. Two other highly coloured versions, *boletus luridus* and *boletus erythropus*, are delicious. Some species are best thrown away as they have an unpleasant taste.

The larger sorts have caps up to twenty centimetres in diameter, sometimes more, and they are all shades of brown, from pale straw colour to chestnut, although one sort is a rather dingy white.

They all have one characteristic in common – their under sides are like very fine sponges with hundreds of tiny pores, that is except the youngest ones which have small, hard, round caps so tightly crimped to their stems that their spongy undersides are invisible. The stems of the *porcini* are thick and squat and bulbous, like the trunks of very old oak trees that have been pollarded. Some sorts have a delicious fungoid smell, others have a nasty smell, others have scarcely any at all.

Neither of us was a stranger to *boleti*. Back in the 1950s we had hunted them (for that is what it feels like, the search for them, a hunt) in the Carso near Trieste, in northern Scotland, on Wimbledon Common, only about eight miles from Hyde Park Corner, and at Wisley in Surrey, exercising all the skill and cunning at our command.

Eventually, we had been forced to abandon Wimbledon Common as we found ourselves hopelessly out-manoeuvred by more cunning, better informed fungus hunters than we were – Czechs and Italians from Soho, and some Russians from their trade enclave in Highgate, who moved in every morning at first light. Skill and cunning are necessary because, in dealing with fungi, particularly *boletus*, you are entering a world in which, having penetrated it, you begin to realize that you are dealing with growths that give every indication of being motivated by some supernatural power. It is said, for example, that if you succeed in finding a *boletus*, and then fail to gather it – it should be cut, not wrenched out by the roots – it will disappear back into the earth from which it was in the act of emerging. If you do pick them they should be put in a basket, never in a plastic bag. The absence of fresh air ruins them.

A few days after the *maltempo* in Tuscany had ended the news spread like wildfire – it was actually in the local newspaper – that there were *funghi* in the mountains and all the *contadini* with any woods to their names, or high meadows in which other sorts of *funghi* grew, immediately made plans to set off to gather them. This was to anticipate the arrival of *raccoglitori* from the city, many of them professional *funghi* gatherers who would already be on their way to the Apennines and the Apuan Alps to strip them of the *funghi* which since time immemorial had been the property of the owners of the woods and meadows, the legal *raccoglitori*. Tempers were already running high and several *padroni* said they would be taking their shotguns with them in case, as they put it, there was an opportunity for '*un po' di caccia*', though what sort of hunting – birds, beasts, the shooting season had already begun, or illegal *raccoglitori di funghi* – was not clear.

It was now, much to our surprise, that we received an invitation from Signor Giuseppe to join him and Signora Fernanda and Signora Angiolina on a *funghi* hunt in some woods on the north side of the Foce il Cuccù, which belonged to them, leaving immediately.

We had not been surprised that we hadn't been invited to take part in their *vendemmia*. Their *vigneto* was of comparatively modest dimensions and there was really no need of any outside help. There was Signora Fernanda's married son and her daughter-in-law, and Signora Fernanda's daughter who had married a shopkeeper in Sarzana and had two teenage daughters.

The invitation to the *funghi* hunt was, however, another matter. They really had no need of assistance and it was really kind of them to do so when the current price was some astronomical number of lire a kilo, although it would fall dramatically if they really began to proliferate. We ourselves were not at all sanguine about the chances of finding any *funghi*. Previous experience had taught us that the more optimistic one was, the less chance one had of finding any at all. Besides, I was still smarting under the humiliation of the affair of the wild asparagus, something which Signora Angiolina still used to remind me about, roguishly, from time to time.

Armed each of us with a knife, a stick for prodding about in the undergrowth and what looked like a far too large number of baskets in which to carry away our spoils, if indeed there were any, we set off in the Land Rover for the Foce il Cuccù, Attilio's mysterious Shangri-la, the secret of which, where beyond it he went to do his famous *giornate*, or for whom, he never ever yielded up.

153

Was it a *padrone* or a *padrona*? He had already declared that Wanda was '*la mia padrona*'. Was Attilio a man with a *padrona* in every port?

The view that morning from the Foce was magnificent. To the south and west, cities, towns, the nearest of which was Fosdinovo with its enormous castle, villages, rivers, seas, offshore islands, gulfs and plains, a whole world in microcosm was visible as in a painting by Leonardo.

And something we had not yet seen, except fleetingly when we first visited Fosdinovo while trying to buy I Castagni, to the north and east was the *crinale*, the high main ridge of the Apennines, on the far side of which I had spent part of the winter of 1943–4, holed up in caves and cabins in the snow.

Below the Foce, on the side facing the Ligurian Sea, the mountain fell away gently to an alpine meadow in which the grass was still green in spite of the time of year, not bleached as it was almost everywhere else, because this was a place where several springs rose to the surface, springs that eventually fed the Magra. Across this verdant expanse a large flock of sheep was grazing its way with infinite slowness, followed by what looked like a semi-somnolent shepherd and his rather more wide-awake dog.

In the midst of this meadow stood a fine old farmhouse with a balcony laden with flowers of a sort that exists everywhere in the north Italian Alps but was something of a rarity here. Here, although it was only 500 metres above the sea, it was too exposed for vines to grow. Here, the following spring, this great green meadow would be carpeted with highly scented narcissi, otherwise known as *i fiori del mal di testa*, headache flowers, because if you sleep with them in your bedroom they are liable to bring on the symptoms of a rather nasty hangover, because of the very strong scent.

Further along the ridge from the Foce to the north-west, also on the side that faced the Magra and the sea, the mountain fell away more steeply and more densely wooded, and it was in the upper part of these dense woods in which the brambles were more than twenty feet long that Renato and his fellow *cacciatori* had let loose the wild boars that, according to reports, were breeding with enthusiasm and would soon be wreaking havoc unless they were culled.

Beyond the Foce we left the vehicle on a little plateau and entered the woods. The trees were chestnuts mostly, their branches bowed under the weight of the nuts that would soon be ready for collecting, that was if anyone was prepared to collect them.

Some of these trees were very old and the bark was so deeply grooved in what were regular spirals that their trunks looked like giant screws embedded in the earth. Some were dying from a disease that caused them to exude a black liquid; others were dead, without bark, wind-blasted, silvery grey skeletons.

Until recently these chestnuts had provided uncountable generations of *contadini* with some of the principal necessities of life: fuel in the form of firewood and charcoal; timber for building materials, furniture and vehicles; food in the form of chestnut flour that was used to make the *castagnaccia*, what had been a staple food that most old *contadini* now wanted to forget they had ever eaten, because of the memories it brought back of long years of poverty.

Here, on the north side of the ridge, the woods were now already in shadow for a large part of the day and at first it was difficult to make out anything at all. Now the track was so heavily overgrown with weeds and brambles that there was absolutely no hope of finding any *funghi*; but after following it around the side of the hill for a mile or so it began to be clearer and we could look down into the woods on our left hand where they plummeted down towards the gorge of a stream that eventually fed the Aulella, and on the right look up into them as they soared away overhead up the steep slope to the ridge.

It was now that Signor Giuseppe suddenly halted and began to root about with his stick, eventually unearthing a small boundary stone, what he called a *cippo*, one of a number that delimited his particular piece of property which altogether must have covered something like a square mile of mountainside uphill from the track on which we were standing. I found this feat extremely impressive as eventually he was able to uncover the other three.

'*Andiamo su!*' he said, and we all began to climb the steep north-facing slope, the idea being that we should first get to the uppermost part of his property at the ridge and then descend, rather than gathering *funghi* on the way up and then having to retrace our steps laden, we hoped, with baskets full of them.

In these operations Signora Angiolina, who always looked as if a puff of wind might blow her to smithereens, displayed uncommon agility and it was she who made the first find of the day as soon as we began to descend from the ridge with the words '*Ecco, ho trovato!*', in this case two *boleti* which were growing in a bed of brilliant green moss at the foot of a *castagno*. They were *boletus badius*, brown with stems and caps of a similar shade of chestnut brown, a sort that Signora Angiolina called *porcinelli*. Her loud cry caused her to be rebuked by Signor Giuseppe who ordered her to keep quiet on the grounds that goodness only knew how many urban *raccoglitori* were loose in the surrounding woods only waiting to hear that Signora Angiolina had lit on some *porcinelli*, before making their attack on the family fungus bed from an undefended flank; but there was no one, not now or at any time during that long day – there was no *merenda* – just the wind sighing in the trees and an occasional squawk from some unidentifiable bird that had somehow managed to remain alive.

It was the most successful *funghi* hunt that we had ever engaged in during all the years we were in Italy. I will always remember the first big *boletus*, also a *porcinello*, I found that day, alone in solitary splendour, unravaged by worms, its cap the size of a small soup plate. They were everywhere. There were varieties I had never seen before, one with a brick-red cap, which our book on the subject said was delicious, another with a coffee-coloured cap and brilliant yellow underparts and a ring round the upper part of the stem, like a sort of veil.

But presiding over all, like the skeletons at a feast of *raccoglitori di funghi*, were *amanita phalloides*, otherwise *amanita verdognola*, death caps, the caps of which exhibit an alarming range of shades of pale olive, greyish-green, yellow and near-white, the most poisonous *funghi* of all. And there was also *amanita virosa*, the destroying angel, which is dead white. Both varieties were out in force. Whoever eats the smallest morsel of either of these is more or less assured of a horrible death. Some of the cures that were attempted in the past were almost as awful as the symptoms – one involved the victim being forced to eat a paste compounded from three hashed stomachs and seven raw brains of rabbits, without any discernible improvement.

Descending the mountainside, looking for *funghi*, what surprised me was how different those woods in the Apennines were when I lived in them, and how different these woods in the Apuan Alps would also have been at that time. Now, apart from a few woodcutters with tractors and trailers, and some *raccoglitori* such as ourselves in the *funghi* season, they were deserted. At this time of year back in 1943, entire families would have been out working in them, loading wood for their own use and for sale on to the wooden sledges drawn by cows or bullocks, or loading it on to mules, singing and shouting to one another as they did so.

And at that time there were charcoal burners in the woods. All of them, and their families if they lived on the site, men, women and children, as black as night from the charcoal. They lived in huts, the roofs covered with boughs and turf, and they slept on beds made with leafy branches. The men who did the burning never left the big, earth-covered cones of tree trunks that looked a bit like wigwams with smoke coming out of the tops of them. The wood had to combust night and day without bursting into flame until the wood was charred through completely.

There were no longer any *carbonari* in this part of Tuscany, few people used charcoal for cooking any more, but the platforms they constructed, dug out of the mountainsides, could still be seen in their hundreds here and almost everywhere else in the mountains of Italy. And if you dug down a few inches in one of these platforms you would be almost certain to find numbers of what looked like oversize pencil leads, which were lengths of pure, combusted charcoal. I found these abandoned settlements very sad. I could remember the way these people looked and the things they said, just as I could remember the things the woodcutters and their families used to say, and I expected to hear them now, but they would never come back.

Now most of the tracks the woodcutters and the charcoal burners had made through the woods all those years ago had grown over. Then, when I was hiding in similar woods in the Apennines, they used to form huge labyrinths of tunnels, filled with light and shade when the sun shone down into them, just as it had done at the place where we had eaten Rina's *merenda* on the first day of the Dadà *vendemmia*.

Using these tunnels I could move across country invisible to anyone more than a few feet away. If the families had brought their dogs with them into the woods it would have been impossible but most of them left their dogs in their farmyards to guard the house, tethered on running wires. These secret journeys continued until the November winds stripped the trees bare and the snow came, *la piccola neve*, the small snow. Then, everyone said, 'When the big snow comes they will take you away.' And they did.

✛

Altogether, after the *funghi* hunt, we had ten large, loaded baskets of assorted *boleti* between the five of us. '*E un fenomeno!*' was how Signor Giuseppe, never at a loss for the right word, described the proceeds of our labours, when we all assembled in his back yard to lay them out for acceptance or rejection.

'*Eccellente!*', '*mangereccio!*', '*mangiabile*' were just some of the complimentary epithets Signor Giuseppe reserved for the *funghi* picked by his own side. They were strictly confined to three sorts: *boletus edulis* (the real *porcino*), *boletus badius* and *boletus scaber*. But some of the others Wanda and I had picked, though undoubtedly *boleti*, he subjected to a particularly severe inspection. '*Sospetto!*' ('suspect!'), '*da gettar via!*' ('to throw away!'), '*velenoso, probabilmente mortale!*' ('poisonous, probably fatal!') were just some of the epithets he heaped on some of the species, such as *boletus luteus*, we had expended much energy in looking for, one of which, *boletus rufus*, was, in the opinion of some experts, even better than *boletus scaber*.

'If we listen to Signor Giuseppe we won't have anything left at all,' Wanda said. 'We've eaten *boletus luteus* for years and personally I'm not going to give up now.' So we didn't.

That evening Wanda cooked them under the grill with olive oil, lemon, salt and pepper, a mixture of those *funghi* that Signor Giuseppe and his family considered to be *commestibili*, and the ones that we knew to be harmless but they were convinced were *velenosi* or *da gettar via*.

The first thing that Signor Giuseppe did the following morning, suspecting quite correctly that Wanda would have wilfully disregarded his various prohibitions, was to send Signora Fernanda down to our house at a hideously early hour to find out if we had already succumbed.

And it was her strident cries of 'SIGNOORA! SIGNOORE! STATE BENE, VOI DUE ANCORA?' ('Are you still all right?') that caused us both to shoot into an upright sitting position, leap out of bed – this time without my capsizing the *vaso da notte* – and tumble down the outside staircase to prove to her, at 5 a.m., that we were not in our death agonies.

All she said when she did finally set eyes on us was '*mosca!*', as if she was ever so slightly disappointed at finding us still alive.

⊹

But in spite of this promising beginning the *funghi* that year never reached anything like the astronomical number that had been predicted. Two days later we went back with Signor Giuseppe and Signora Fernanda and found none at all. It was not only in their part of the woods. It was the same everywhere. Like Attilio, the *funghi* had simply decided to make no further appearance. It was as if they had taken fright in the face of so many ruthless hunters, being by nature timid but determined creatures who did not enjoy having their roots plucked from the earth, and had therefore disappeared, fearing total extinction, to whence they came, leaving behind a suicide squad composed of the terrible *amanita phalloides* with a sprinkling of destroying angels to annihilate as many of their persecutors as possible.

From now on, whenever *funghi* were in season, which could be from spring to late autumn, according to the terrain, the sort of *funghi* and the weather conditions, Wanda prepared them in a variety of ways. She was inspired by Rina and by her own favourite cookery book, Pellegrino Artusi's *La Scienza in Cucina o L'Arte di Mangiar Bene*, by that time in its thirty-ninth edition.

She cooked the other edible varieties, *boletus* mostly, *in umido* with garlic and parsley, oil and tomatoes, a Ligurian dish; and as a risotto, and *fritti*, cooked in olive oil, with salt and pepper. And all through the year they could be used dried.

The only person we knew who wouldn't eat *funghi*, whether prepared by Wanda or anyone else, even Signora Angiolina, was Attilio.

'*Non mi piacciono. Non li voglio*,' he used to say when Wanda offered him a delicious plateful, as a courtesy, knowing that he would refuse. '*Vuol favorire*, Attilio?'

'Sometimes,' Wanda used to say to me after one of the quiet but determined refusals, 'I begin to wonder if he refuses because he really is a fungus in disguise. With that pale cap on he looks a bit like one. The sort that grows in fir woods and goes blue when you cut it up and is very good to eat. I can't remember the name.'

We looked it up in our pocket book on the subject, *Funghi* by Pierre Montarnal, our constant companion in the field. It was *boletus cyanescens*, the one that goes blue when you cut it up, described by the author as *molto apprezzato*. 'Perhaps we ought to saw Attilio in half and see if he goes blue,' I said. 'Or perhaps you ought to do it. After all you are *la sua padrona*, his boss.'

'If only you knew,' she said, 'how frightened it makes me being his *padrona*. It's a bit like having Einstein as a son-in-law.'

✝

A few years later when *sagre*, non-religious festivals mostly connected with food and drink, were all the rage – there were *sagre* of anything from pancakes to eels – a great *Sagra del Fungo*, fungus feast, was held at Casciano Petrosa, a small, lonely village on a very winding road which eventually deposited the traveller in the marble quarries above Carrara in the Apuan Alps.

The *sagra* began at nine in the morning with a celebration of a Mass which it seemed to us a wise form of life assurance to attend. This was followed by the opening of an exhibition in which drawings of *funghi*, made by local schoolchildren, were displayed and actual examples of poisonous and non-poisonous varieties found in the region, one of the richest in *funghi* anywhere in Italy in a normal year, were also on show.

At eleven o'clock the Director of Pathology and Microbiology at Pisa University rose to his feet and gave a rather long talk, as directors of anything in Italy tend to do. After this he, the committee and other important guests of whom there were inexhaustible supplies, sat down to a protracted luncheon. At three o'clock, by which time the hoi polloi, ourselves included, were becoming impatient, a truly enormous *degustazione* of *.funghi* began. This orgy, for which a very nominal charge was made, and in the course of which great quantities of not very good wine were drunk, took place under the trees of the courtyard of what was a very rustic inn.

There the *funghi*, *porcini* for the first course, *clavaria* for the second, a sort we had never seen before, let alone eaten, were fried in batter in an outsize iron frying pan three and a half feet in diameter, over an open fire, by men and women of the village working in relays.

The *clavaria botrytis* which came in the second fry-up were really extraordinary-looking growths. They had trunks and branches with pink tips and looked exactly like coral. They were delicious. Another, very similar, *clavaria fumosa*, according to our book had a laxative effect and was not on the menu.

And copious though the quantity of *funghi* was on offer at this *sagra* in Casciano Petrosa it was such a bad year for *funghi* all

161

over Italy that the organizers almost had to cancel the event, whereas in a good year the inhabitants said the *funghi* would have been arriving in wagon-loads.

The winter that followed our *funghi* hunt was the one in which our mice, sleek from a long summer in the fields, took possession of I Castagni and started their re-furnishing programme by using my favourite red flannel shirt to make bedcovers for their children in one of our chests-of-drawers, which they used as a dormitory whenever we were not in occupation of the house. From then on everything of any value we possessed, which included the mattresses for the beds, had to be parcelled up in thick nylon and hung from the ceilings on wires when the house was unoccupied.

✠

One of the few events we were never able to take part in during all the time we were at I Castagni, something we were sorry to miss, although it was really rather a boring job, was the *raccolta d'olive*, the olive harvest.

This was because it took place during the winter months and was a much more protracted affair than the grape harvest. It could also be cold work. Many people used to carry copper heaters fuelled with charcoal into the fields in order to restore their circulation. One year it was so cold that a lot of the trees split and for some time subsequently the crop was much diminished.

With the number of weeks holiday I was eligible for each year the choice really came between taking them between spring and autumn, when we could do our own *vendemmia* (which was one of the principal reasons for having the place), and helping other families with theirs (which was half the fun of being there); or spending part of the winter at I Castagni and helping with the olive harvest. There was, in fact, when it came to it, no choice because in my job the winter months until after Christmas were the busiest of all.

In fact, all I was ever able to do, so far as the olives were concerned, was to weed and dig the earth around our own trees, which was quite a big job as by the end of the summer the ground was usually iron hard.

It was Signor Giuseppe and Signora Fernanda who actually harvested the olives and it was from them, when we returned in the spring, that we received, with some ceremony, a share of the oil after it had been pressed, which always made us feel both feudal and slightly uncomfortable, having done next to nothing to produce it.

However much oil there was, it was never enough for Wanda's needs and almost always we had to make a special journey into the country around Montecarlo out beyond Lucca in order to buy more to take back to England.

Chapter Sixteen

ONE OF THE REASONS why I had looked forward to living at I Castagni was that I would be able to return to the Apennines and retrace my steps along the part of the *crinale*, its main ridge, that I had last traversed when I had been escaping.

The Apennines are not particularly impressive in their early stages at their northern end above the Italian Riviera; but in the section which separates the province of Massa Carrara in Tuscany from the provinces of Parma and Emilia they become altogether wilder and higher with peaks rising to over 6000 feet.

This was the section of the Apennines I could see from the Foce il Cuccù above Fosdinovo in what I called Attilio land: snow-covered in winter; swathed in heat haze in summer; often cloud-covered at any season and prone to violent electric storms which made it extremely dangerous to be on it.

Although I was very keen to do the walk, Wanda was not very happy about my doing it alone, and I wasn't really very happy about it either. There are dense forests on the far, cold, northern side of the *crinale*, in which I still vividly remembered getting lost during the war in 1943. You only had to break or sprain an ankle in one of these forests and be immobilized and no one would ever find you. Everyone tells you to take a whistle when entering such country but my experience with whistles was that they had a surprisingly short range, especially if any sort of wind was blowing. Anyway, I would look pretty stupid, as travel editor of a national newspaper, if I disappeared and became the subject of a large-scale search.

Then one day I had a lucky encounter with a couple of forest guards in a town called Pontrémoli. Pontrémoli was then a rather old-fashioned town of about five thousand inhabitants on the upper waters of the Magra at its confluence with a lesser stream, the Torrente Verde.

It has a deep, almost canyon-like main street lined with old *palazzi*, which terminates in a couple of *piazze*, separated from one another by the Torre dell'Orologio, part of a fortress known in the dialect as '*al campanun*', 'the bell', built by the ubiquitous Castruccio Castracani in 1332 in order to separate the Guelfs and the Ghibellines, the two rival factions in the town, and prevent them cutting one another's throats, one of the few things they really enjoyed doing.

When I discussed with the two *guardie*, who were each about thirty years of age, what had already begun to seem the problem of finding a suitable companion for the walk they immediately offered to come with me, providing their commanding officer had no objections. They didn't anticipate any trouble from him as this particular part of the Apennines was in their territory anyway, and they could make it a routine patrol. In fact they told me that neither of them had ever walked all of it.

They said we should take crampons, which they would be able to provide, as there would probably still be quite a lot of frozen snow on the ridges, and that I should provide a compass, as they hadn't got one. I also decided to take my discredited whistle with me, but without telling them.

Altogether, they said, if we weren't stormbound, we should do the whole thing from the Passo di Lagastrello to the Passo della Cisa in one long day and part of the next one. There was no mountaineering involved. It was just a hill walk.

I already had the maps, the 1:25,000 editions published by the Istituto Geografico Militare which at that time were only published in black-and-white. They were very detailed (there were eleven different conventional signs for trees) and looked as if they had been drawn by a *scarafaggio* with inky feet. If going any distance you needed a lot of them but at least they were cheap.

Two days later Wanda drove me up to Rigoso, a very windswept village with big beech woods looming over it, 1131 metres up on the Parma side of the Passo di Lagastrello, on the road from Aulla to Parma. From it, if everything had not been blotted out by cloud, I would have been able to see the Alpe di Succiso, 2017 metres, the highest peak in the next section of the *crinale*, away to the south-east, but I couldn't. 'Take care, my writer,' Wanda said, which was more or less what I said to her, driving in thick cloud down the steep side of the Apennines back to Fosdinovo in a Land Rover.

In Rigoso I slept in one of three modest inns, all of which were equally clean, friendly and decent, but I can now no longer remember which one as I had a rather wild night with the forest guards, Giovanni and Pietro, in the course of which we visited all three of them.

The following morning at seven o'clock, feeling rather fragile, we set off for the *crinale*. The weather was terrible too, with heavy rain and all the hill and mountain tops covered with cloud; but in spite of this the guards decided to make for Monte Malpasso, the first major eminence on the *crinale* at 1716 metres, by way of a glacial lake, one of fourteen such lakes strung out along the foot of the ridge on its cold eastern side.

The next three quarters of an hour through sodden beech woods to the lake at 1241 metres in what was now sleet, and then to Monte Malpasso in another hour and a half, were awful.

There was hard snow all along the ridge and deep pockets of it on the cold east side. There was no point in climbing Monte Malpasso as it was swaddled in cloud and the wind was very strong, so we continued round the side of it through beech woods, passing some stone shepherds' huts. Some of the huts had strange, primitive carvings of sheep on their lintels and on the stones lying about outside them. They would remain empty until the sheep were brought up sometime in June.

At around 11 a.m. we reached Monte Bocco, 1791 metres, a

grass-grown peak rising from the ridge and falling sheer into Lunigiana on the Tuscan side, with a good deal of snow around the foot of it.

For the next few miles, the ridge was a grassy, icy switchback with every so often a peak rising from it, rather like a giant tooth: Monte Bragalata, 1835 metres, Monte Losanna, 1856 metres, and the Passo di Compione with a mule track leading down to a collection of huts of the same name in Lunigiana, all of which was now completely concealed by a grey void of cloud.

About five hours out from Rigoso we reached Monte Sillara, 1861 metres, the highest peak in this section of the Apennines. At this moment the sun came out and we decided to climb it.

From the top it was almost as if you could see for ever: on one hand down to the Pianura Padana, the great plain of the Po, on the other the Gulf of Spezia, the valley of the Magra and the Apuan Alps; and to the south a big tract of the Apennines, peak after peak. To the north there was the whole of the Alpine chain, much of it still snow-covered, extending from Monviso, on the frontier between France and Italy where the Po rises, to the Dolomites.

While admiring these astonishing vistas, the second time in my life I had done so, we ate bread and *prosciutto* and chocolate, and drank cold red wine. The trouble was that it was very, very cold. Far too cold to be sitting on a rock admiring the view. 'We should have brought a bottle of *grappa*,' Pietro, the smaller of the two, said. Then it clouded over and it was colder than ever. It was time to go.

At 1.15 p.m. we reached Monte Matto, 1837 metres. It was from the summit of Monte Matto, in the late autumn of 1943, that I had looked down on the Passo di Badignana, a 1685-metre pass that linked the province of Parma with that of Massa Carrara, and seen columns of men, women, children and pack mules climbing up to it. Those from Massa Carrara, as I subsequently learned, were bringing olive oil and salt; those from Parma bringing all sorts of food to exchange at the pass, transporting these commodities in little handcarts, on pack mules and in backpacks.

At that time I was living in a cave that the people of a village called Lalatta had constructed for me on the side of a mountain called Monte Cajo. It had taken me ten and a half hours hard walking to reach Monte Matto from Monte Cajo and I had made the journey to see if there was any chance of my reaching the coast south of La Spezia and being taken off by a British submarine which was supposed to be operating somewhere along it; but, of course, there wasn't. That night, lost in a dense forest on the cold face of the *crinale*, I met the old man I confused with Attilio.

But now it all seemed a dream, what I had seen from Monte Matto, *matto* meaning mad, something that had never happened, never been. And I looked at Giovanni and Pietro – who I had been glad to discover were not all that fit – and wondered what they would have done if they had been forest guards in the service of what was then a Fascist administration, and they had met me up there. Would they have handed me over to their employers, or to the Germans – that is if they hadn't shot me out of hand with their carbines – or would they have hidden me and helped me? The last forest guard I had seen was on the way to Monte Matto. He was an ugly-looking customer and I had been told that if he saw me he would take me; but fortunately, he didn't see me.

Now, there was not much to see at the Passo di Badignana. A long, slender pole stuck in the ground to mark its whereabouts was oscillating in the wind that was funnelling up to it from the Tuscan side, just as its twin had done when I had been there previously. Today the wind was bringing up great puffs of black cloud with it as if someone far below in Treschietto, a village I had already visited with Wanda, had lit a great fire burning some noxious substance. Here at the pass we got water from a spring called the Fontana del Vescovo, the Bishop's Spring.

The next part, after the Passo di Badignana, was the most exciting of the entire walk. From now on, for a considerable distance, the *crinale* was a real knife-edge. Here, one mis-step to the left and you would fall without a single bounce into the head of some Tuscan valley that had chestnuts, vines and olives growing in it. On the other side, facing the Adriatic, there were beech forests, oaks, some chestnuts, and in some places, larch. There were no olive trees and vines could only be grown in the foothills.

On this side the *crinale* fell away between rocky outcrops, sometimes in long screes of pale, silvery grey stones and slabs speckled with yellowish lichen. These marked the upper limits of the alpine meadows in which the sheep grazed in summer and the shepherds had their huts.

Here, beyond the Passo di Badignana, the track on the *crinale* took us along the outer edge of what was a wind-blasted, impenetrable wood of dwarf beeches, the only trees that would grow at such a height, and they looked as if their upper branches had been sawn off diagonally with a hedgecutter.

Somehow these trees had succeeded in reaching the knife-edge at around 1700 metres, from the cold side of the *crinale*, rooting themselves in what looked like solid rock on the way, and partially engulfing the only track along it among the rocks, which was here not more than a foot wide. Forced to abandon it we had to walk along the edge of what was an abyss on the Tuscan side filled with swirling black cloud. The wind was tremendous and it constantly changed direction, buffeting us from all sides. I began to wish we had brought a rope.

At 3.30 p.m. we reached Monte Brusà, 1796 metres, still in very thick weather, and the Passo della Guadine, 1680 metres, at 4 p.m. Nearby a boundary stone, a bit more grand than Signor Giuseppe's in his *fungaia*, carved with their coats of arms, marked the division between the territory of the Grand Duke of Tuscany on one hand and that of Maria Luigia, Duchess of Parma, on the other. She was Napoleon's second wife, the mother of the King of Rome and the daughter of Francis I of Austria, who was given the Duchy to rule in 1816 as a result of one of the more happy decisions arrived at during the Congress of Vienna. Her reign was a felicitous one.

At 4.30 p.m. we reached Monte dell'Aquila, 1707 metres, in what was now pouring rain and a hellish wind. All three of us were beginning to feel pretty miserable, especially as night appeared to be falling although it was the end of the first week in May, and I began to see why my two friends didn't make a practice of visiting the *crinale*.

At 5 p.m. we got to the Passo dell'Aquila and began the descent on the Parma side to a *rifugio* at the Lago Santo in which the guards had arranged for the three of us to spend the night. All the way down to it we talked about what we were going to eat and drink when we finally arrived there. Roast lamb had been ordered for the main course and the Signora was known to be a notable cook. There was even the possibility of hot baths.

Plodding down this rain-sodden track it was difficult to believe that in a month or two bilberries and wild raspberries would be flourishing here, and in a very few weeks all sorts of *funghi* also. We got to the *rifugio* just after 6 p.m., by which time it was quite dark. The walk had taken us eleven and a half hours from Rigoso.

Awaiting us at the *rifugio* was a young village priest. He was the bearer of a message from a village whose inhabitants had kept me alive during the war. One of those who had helped me was a man named Silvestre Agnosini who had hidden me and a boon companion, also an escaping prisoner, in his hut high up on the sides of a mountain called Monte Fageto, at a height of 1200 metres. When I first knew him Signor Silvestre was almost blind. Now he was totally blind.

Wanda and I had already made plans to visit him and the other people who had helped me the following week, and those in another couple of villages in the vicinity, something we had been doing for years every time we were in the Apennines, but it was too complicated to do the walk and the visit at the same time.

Without preamble the priest, a young man, said that I must come with him immediately to the village to visit Signor Silvestre who, apparently, had learned by a sort of bush telegraph that I was in the neighbourhood and would be extremely upset if I didn't come at once.

I was angry at the way the priest had presented the matter and at the same time I felt ashamed at even hesitating to do what he was asking me to do. It was useless to say that I was coming to see Silvestre and the others the following week.

I said that of course I would come. We all had a *grappa*, including the priest, and then the two of us set off for the village which was called Vecciatica. It took three quarters of an hour by a steep and rocky track, the continuation of the one by which we had come down from the *crinale*, to get to the place where the road began and the priest had left his car, using torches as the night was as black as pitch and the rain was hissing down; it took another half an hour by car to get to Vecciatica.

Signor Silvestre used to make the long, arduous journey up to the hut every day bringing food, that was if it wasn't snowing, a long hard climb. Sometimes one of his young sons would accompany him, or his daughter. Sometimes he came by himself.

When he arrived he used to sit down in front of the fire and say, 'Now let us talk about New York', or 'Let us talk about New Guinea', or wherever it was he wanted to talk about, and then one or other of us two *Inglesi* would turn the log on which he was sitting to what we hoped was the direction of wherever it was and when he was properly orientated we would begin to talk about these places, most of which we were as ignorant about as he was.

Then, at Christmas, we went down through the snow to spend Christmas with him and his wife and the other people of the village who had helped us. Signor Grassi, who mended my boots after I burned a hole through the sole when I fell asleep by the fire in the hut, and his wife; and Signor Valenti and his wife, Luisa, who gave us each a hot bath in a big wine barrel and washed our hair; and Signor Soldati, who was a carpenter, and his wife, and many others.

And so, when I finally reached Vecciatica, with the rain still pouring down, still soaked through, there had been no point in changing, and knocked on the door of Signor Silvestre's house which was the last in the village, and said, '*Permesso?*' as I always had, and it opened and he stood there, with his hands outstretched with the signora standing behind him, looking over his shoulder, and he said, '*Ti stavo aspettando,* Enrico' ('I have been waiting for you'), I knew that my journey had been really necessary.

✠

The following day, after waiting hours for the weather to improve, which it didn't, we left around nine. We didn't really mind because we were all feeling a bit battered. Outside it was as thick as porridge.

The next obstacle was Monte Orsaro, 1831 metres, 400 metres overhead in what the Germans call the *Ewigkeit*, the eternity. It took us an hour and a half to get to it by way of Lago Padre, another minute glacial lake, and the Bocchetta dell'Orsaro, a very nasty windswept break in the *crinale* at 1821 metres. The final climb of what looked quite like a real rocky mountain, with visibility about thirty feet, was rather difficult as Monte Orsaro was the nodal point of a number of ridges leading down from it in various directions, all except one of which would land us in the soup.

It was at this time, having entrusted the map and the compass to Pietro, under the impression that he was *au fait* with how to use them, that I discovered that he wasn't. He took the wrong ridge. One could hardly blame him.

From Monte Fosco, 1683 metres, to Monte Tavola, 1604 metres, the going was the toughest of the entire trip, by way of something the maps called I Ronchi di Luciano, whatever that was, through a dense forest of beech. There was no track through the forest at all. The only way to pass through it without being lost was to follow what remained of a rusty wire fence which sometimes ceased to exist altogether.

From here onwards there was another difficult section through more of these sodden sodding beech woods to the Passo di Cirone, 1255 metres, which linked Bosco on the Parma side with Pràcchiola, a beautiful Alpine village on the Pontrémoli side of the *crinale*.

The rest was easy, mostly a switchback over downland dotted with trees, but with heavy rain and nil visibility, to the Passo della Cisa, 1039 metres, with the road from Parma to Pontrémoli crossing it, a route followed by Hannibal.

At the Cisa we got a lift to Pontrémoli and squelching in through the main gate to where Wanda was waiting for us we made a rather sorry spectacle.

'I was worried,' were Wanda's first words when we arrived at the *ristorante* where she had been waiting a couple of hours. '*Anche noi,*' Pietro said. 'We also.'

After that I did a number of walks on the *crinale* on various parts of it, one of them alone, but I never again encountered such conditions.

Chapter Seventeen

OUR NEAREST TOWN besides Fosdinovo was Sarzana and we often travelled there on the bus, which was the means by which various ladies, such as Signora Fernanda, conveyed their produce to the market there. Sarzana succeeded Luni, after its destruction and abandonment, as the principal city of the plain and it was then known as Luna Nova.

Originally a possession of the Bishops of Luni, in 1204 they transferred themselves to Sarzana where they exercised their temporal power until 1308. It then became a bone of contention between Pisans who were the first to fortify it, Luccans, Florentines, it was Lorenzo the Magnificent who ordered the building of the present citadel and walls, the Viscontis, the French and the Genoese, and involved matters of such complexity that it would be tedious to attempt to enlarge on them here.

Sarzana was the birthplace of the humanist Pope, Nicholas V, originally Tommaso Parentucelli, who reigned from 1447 to 1455 and in 1450–1 established Glasgow University by Papal Bull. He also organized a crusade against the Turks after the fall of Constantinople in 1453 and acted as an international arbiter when he conferred on Portugal the discoveries made by Henry the Navigator. There was a statue of him on the façade of the cathedral, a position which he shared with two other popes, S. Eutichianus and Sergius IV.

The way into Sarzana, that was if you didn't arrive by way of

Attilio's back road, or by bus, was through a splendid ornamental gateway, made in the fifteenth-century walls of the town in 1783. Once inside it, the Via Mazzini, the principal street, led to the first of the three largest squares, the Piazza Garibaldi, where there was an elegant, early nineteenth-century theatre, the Teatro degli Impavidi (the Fearless), now used as a cinema. At the opposite end of it, where a tree-lined road led down to the railway station and the fruit and vegetable market, there was a huge, nude Carrara marble statue of a man, of vaguely Fascist inspiration, that must have weighed several tons.

Continuing on down Via Mazzini the shops, as the years passed, became progressively more elegant, and we always wondered who actually bought the clothes that were on sale as we never saw anyone wearing them. Certainly no one would ever dream of wearing such garments up the hill at Fosdinovo. What was even more surprising in later years was the proliferation of shops selling chocolates, expensive pastries and eventually luxurious foreign foods, caviar, foie gras, Scotch smoked salmon, and the costliest French wines such as Romanée Conti, Krug and Chateau d'Yquem. I sometimes wondered what Signor Giuseppe would make of a bottle of Romanée Conti.

A short distance further on, on the right, Via Mazzini opened up in Piazza Nicolò V to display the brilliantly white Gothic Cattedrale di S. Maria Assunta, begun in 1340, which then took another 134 years to complete. High up in it, there was a crucifix brought to it from Luni in 1204, painted and signed by the artist, Maestro Guglielmo. And nearby, in the twelfth-century church of San Francesco there was the tomb of Guarniero Antelminelli, son of the omnipresent Castruccio Castracani, erected in 1328.

Continuing on past various *palazzi*, the names of which made I Castagni sound pretty homely, such as Palazzo Piceddi-Benettini and Palazzo Magni-Griffi, whoever they were, we used to pass S. Andrea, the oldest church, first recorded in 1135, with a tall campanile soaring over it. Soon after this Via Mazzini came to an end on the corner of the tree-lined Piazza Matteotti with a huge First World War memorial taking up a lot of space at the lower end where the Palazzo Municipale was, which also took more than eighty years to build, from 1472 to 1554. At this corner there was Sarzana's poshest *caffè* in which some of the older, more elegant, slightly grizzled Sarzanesi used to lounge around with camel-hair coats slung insouciantly over their shoulders in the cold weather, reading the papers and indulging in various other cultural works, such as smoking Dunhill pipes.

Behind this square in an old, decrepit part of the town, there were ground floor rooms crammed with junk, a lot of it ironwork, in which Wanda made some interesting finds, that was until richer, more sophisticated *antiquari* from Lucca moved in and it became impossible to buy anything at a reasonable price.

Market day in Sarzana was Thursday. The market took up every inch of space in Piazza Garibaldi, Piazza Matteotti, and the surrounding streets. It was not a very interesting market, apart from being a large one, but everyone, including ourselves, used to go to it, just in case we missed something worth having but nothing even faintly interesting, apart from food, ever turned up.

What we really looked forward to was going to a pizzeria which had an enormous oven and eating pizza and *focaccia*, a delicious sort of flat bread baked and eaten with olive oil, and drinking the rough wine that was all the proprietors had to offer.

✣

And there was Carrara, ruled by the Malaspina, as was Massa for some 317 years from 1473 until 1790, situated at the feet of the great cliffs of the Apuan Alps in which the marble quarries were. Carrara was not only the place where the Mafia and the Camorra ordered their tombstones and sculptors such as Henry Moore chose their materials. It was and is still famous as being the headquarters of the anarchists of the world, could it be because there was so much high explosive lying around? Every year they used to arrive here from all over the world for great get-togethers which were usually of a surprisingly mild kind.

Sometimes, well into the twentieth century, the blocks of marble, having been roughly squared off on the spot, were simply rolled down the mountainside; but usually they were lowered down a series of paved slipways on wooden sledges, which ran on soaped wooden rollers, their descent controlled by cables wound round posts on either side of the slipways. This was an extremely hazardous business. At the bottom, the blocks were loaded on to ox-wagons and carried off either to the ships at Marina di Massa, or to the railway.

One of the largest of these monoliths quarried at Carrara, perhaps the largest, was 17 metres high, 2.35 metres thick and weighed 300 tons. It was subsequently erected in the Foro Italico, previously the Foro alia Farnesiana, in Rome in 1929.

☩

During our twenty-five years at I Castagni we had innumerable guests. Among the most welcome were those who had been prisoners-of-war in Italy. One of these, Tony Davies, had made a spectacular escape together with another POW, jumping from a train at night while it was on the move, a dangerous thing to do.

He had recently suffered a coronary but in spite of this he succeeded, while staying with us, in climbing the Monte Malpasso, the 1716-metre peak on the *crinale*, along which, almost thirty years earlier, he had walked all the way to the battle front, only to be wounded and re-captured in sight of the Allied front line.

It was unfortunate for his wife, who was terrified of snakes, that the mountainside was infested with adders. Since birds of prey had been for the most part eliminated from the Italian countryside by the *cacciatori*, they had proliferated. Now they literally rose up around her, and around the rest of us – we were not all that happy about them either – and she begged us to order a helicopter to take her off the mountain, a service which we were unable to provide.

Chapter Eighteen

ONE OF THE THINGS we used to look forward to when we were at I Castagni, especially when our children and friends were staying with us, was to travel to Lucca by train.

This rather amazing railway ran from Aulla on the Magra to Lucca, on the way crossing the watershed which separates the Apennines and the Apuan Alps. This line was not finally completed until some time in the early 1960s, by which time in Britain the diabolical Doctor, later Baron Beeching, was proposing the closure of 5000 miles of track, 2000 stations and the dismissal of 70,000 staff, a target he very nearly reached, and would have done, if there had not been a change of government.

To reach one of the numerous stations on this railway, some at a distance of not more than three or four kilometres from one another, we used to drive from Fosdinovo over the Foce il Cuccù and then descend by winding roads which ran through groves of chestnuts and olives, vineyards and small villages such as Tendola, San Terenzo and Ceserano to Rometta, a small place on the far bank of the Aulella, a torrent which feeds the Magra, in which the washing used to hang flapping in the wind like flags. Here we used to leave our vehicle outside the station which was called Stazione Fivizzano–Rometta–Soliera, because these were the principal places which it served, and there at Rometta, we used to buy our return tickets.

Altogether there were about ten trains a day between Aulla and

Lucca, the distance was about 90 kilometres, and the journey took 1 hour 45 minutes, but if you boarded the train at Rometta it took about an hour and a half and was about 10 kilometres shorter.*

Sometimes we left I Castagni an hour or so earlier so that we could visit Fivizzano, a town eight kilometres from Rometta up the valley of the Torrente Rosaro.

Fivizzano was a strange place. Built on a spur of Monte Tergogliano, more than a thousand feet up, until the beginning of the twelfth century its defence was the responsibility of whoever occupied the Castello di Verrúcola, an impressive fortress that looked down on the village of the same name and on Fivizzano itself a couple of hundred feet below.

For the next six hundred years or so the inhabitants of Fivizzano seem to have had an awful time of it. In 1317 the town was badly knocked about by the troops of the *condottiero* Castruccio Castracani who appears to have wreaked havoc wherever and whenever he came on the scene. It then fell into the hands of the Malaspina and in 1430 it was taken by another noted *condottiero*, Piccinino. Almost everyone who arrived at Fivizzano succeeded in damaging it, more or less seriously.

In 1433 Cosimo de' Medici, Cosimo the Elder, built the present walls and used Fivizzano as a base from which to conduct a war against the Republic of Lucca. Extensive damage was caused to it by Charles VIII of France when he entered Italy at the head of an army in 1494. Damage was again done to the town by the troops of the Marchese del Vasto in the sixteenth century, by an earthquake in 1920, and in the Second World War.

The piazza in the centre of what is left of old Fivizzano is entered through a grand archway, and a large part of it is taken up by a splendid fountain erected by Cosimo III in 1683. In it there also stands an elegant sanctuary of 1576, one of the buildings badly shaken by the earthquake but now restored. There is also an *albergo/ristorante*, Il Giardinetto, and an old-fashioned *caffè* which at that time had potted plants in its front window

* Train enthusiasts must excuse any mistakes in my recollections of the railway.

and was always packed with male customers whatever the time of day.

Outside, at what, when we came here before the train left, was an early hour, the streets were more or less deserted. If it was early in the year Fivizzano was a cold place, and if you turned right after emerging from the *caffè* having drunk a *rhum caldo*, you found yourself in a street in which the wind always seemed to be whistling straight down it off the Apennines at the Passo di Lagastrello which in early spring were often covered in snow.

In this street, on the right-hand side there was a building which housed a fantastic collection of ecclesiastical bric-a-brac: candelabra still wreathed in what looked like original spiders' webs, worm-eaten pews, life-size saints in glass cases, pulpits, spooky-looking reliquaries with bits of what had been human beings in them, altar pieces, crumbling bibles and missals, all objects taken from churches that were, one could only hope, no more, and all for sale.

The business was owned by an elderly man who always followed us around to make sure that none of us made off with a reliquary containing a toenail that once belonged to some early Christian martyr, or some such treasure.

He was also an undertaker, an *impresario di pompe funebri* was his correct title, and he had a grandson of about twelve who, he told us, was learning the business, embalming and suchlike, in the holidays and in the evenings when he had finished his homework. A nice hobby for a schoolboy.

The coffins, of which there were dozens, were painted jet-black and were built to last a lifetime, with solid brass handles. The coffins were kept hidden behind long black draperies and sometimes when the double doors on to the street were opened, a sudden gust of wind would part them and display this ghastly collection. Then the old man would become annoyed, as he liked to keep his other interests as a purveyor of religious bric-a-brac separate from that of an *impresario di pompe funebri* in which the supply of coffins appeared to be running in excess of demand (Fivizzano only had 1469 inhabitants at the last count in

1959 and the numbers were still shrinking). What the impresario really needed was a re-run of the Black Death.

Further up this street, on the left, there was an almost equally remarkable establishment, a men's outfitters crammed with hundreds of pairs of trousers, mostly made from synthetic material in the style of the 1950s, with shirts to match, all presided over by a rather grumpy, middle-aged man – living in Fivizzano seemed to make people bad-tempered – who stood in the far corner of the shop, waiting for buyers who never came.

How he himself came into possession of such a quantity of unsaleable clothing was a mystery. The travelling salesman who had succeeded in landing him with them must have been possessed of exceptional powers. Perhaps he had been the travelling salesman.

In order to ingratiate myself with him I eventually bought a pair of his trousers which were surprisingly expensive, considering the horrible material in which they were constructed and the number of years he must have had them in stock. Like antiques they appeared to increase in value with age. They also had the terrible, ineradicable defect of being, as tailors say, 'cut too high in the rise', which gives the wearer the impression that his private parts are dragging along the ground.

But in spite of my efforts to drum up some trade it was no use. He still found my presence just as irritating as if I hadn't bought anything. All he was interested in was a complete clearance – and the next time we went to visit him he locked the door in our faces. The time after that neither he nor his stock was there any more and we were told he was *defunto*. Perhaps he is buried somewhere on the southern slopes of the Apennines under a huge pile of trousers.

☩

Back at the station, we waited for the train. For a long time, from the moment it left Aulla, we could hear it howling as it came, with the driver of what was now, in the second half of the twentieth century, a diesel engine pulling out the stops on what was the equivalent of an old-fashioned train whistle, which now sounded as if someone was being conveyed by ambulance to a casualty ward.

When it came in – Stazione Fivizzano–Rometta–Soleria was the first stop – we leapt aboard, clutching the baskets which contained our *merenda* and which, later, empty by this time, we would use for our shopping in Lucca. Then the stationmaster, or sometimes his wife if he was elsewhere, waved a baton at the driver and we were off. All three of them liked us to make use of their train, especially at this off-peak time of day when any workers who used it were long since at work and no one was due to travel in the other direction for hours yet. By doing so we became a statistic in favour of the continuation of the service which, if some Italian version of Beeching appeared on the scene, could be very uncertain. In fact no such reformer did appear and, at the time of writing, the service continues. Altogether, besides ourselves, there were not usually more than half a dozen passengers on the train at any one time, except on the return journey and in the school summer holidays, which in Italy go on for ever.

But it was more fun when there were other locals on board. Then we could talk about the weather if it merited it, the crops, the prospects for the *vendemmia* and always, never forgetting, the State of Italy.

Now the train entered a short tunnel and emerged from it to cross the Aulella. The countryside was beautiful as it was everywhere all along the line, with little villages and towers and castles and churches perched on hills and crags, and vines and olives and cypresses and chestnuts flourishing, and there were farmhouses down near the line with peasants working in the shade of the trees and the *pergole*, just as they would be at this time of day around I Castagni on the other side of the mountains; and when we waved to them they waved back. And there were pastoral scenes that resembled paintings by Claude or Poussin, and some of them were almost as good.

It was difficult looking out at such scenes to believe that in this area, in August 1944, the SS had massacred 369 persons, mostly women and children, some of them in the villages we had passed through on the way from Fosdinovo to the station, and destroyed a total of 454 houses, as a reprisal for attacks on the 16th Reichsführer Division. And that in the course of this operation the entire family of Renato, our bricklayer – father, mother, brothers and sisters – were all murdered, he, then a small boy, being the only survivor.

Here we went through a short tunnel and looming overhead now, their high peaks hidden in a dark blue indigo haze which only allowed us to see their outline indistinctly, were the Apuan Alps. Now, having crossed the Aulella, the train abandoned it and began to punch its way up the valley of another torrent, the Lucido.

Meanwhile we sat, weather permitting with the windows open, eating our *merenda* of bread and *prosciutto* and drinking our red wine. If there were any other *contadini* sitting close to us on the train, custom demanded that we should offer to share our picnic with them – '*Vuol favorire?*' – and if they had any food that they were going to eat on the journey, they would offer it to us; but such offers were not really expected to be accepted, and seldom were. Quite often it rained and there was a thick fog and the whole scene looked like a wet day in Ballachulish, but it was with the heat and the sun and the blue indigo haze that we both like to remember it.

After seventeen kilometres – you could tell how far you had come by looking out of the window and consulting the kilometre stones – we reached Stazione Monzone–Monte Bianchi–Isolano, and then at twenty kilometres the station for Équi Terme. Équi Terme was at that time a wonderfully dotty and primitive spa. Much patronized by local people it stood on the banks of the Lucido, in which there was usually very little water, unless the snow was melting up in the Alps, or there had been a storm. The old baths, which were probably in use in Roman times, were at the foot of a cliff on the far bank. Its waters, which were terribly smelly, were laced with *cloruro solfato-sodico*, what sounded a nasty mixture of chlorine, sulphur and sodium, and it first emerged from the bowels of the earth, so far as we could ascertain after digging about in it, a short way up the torrent, staining everything it came in touch with in various virulent shades of yellow.

The Terme had a very nice, modest, old-fashioned, slightly Firbankian hotel, the Albergo Radium, which had some good nineteenth-century furniture, and was open from 15 May to 15 October, by which date it was pretty empty.

According to the prospectus, obtainable from the Albergo, these waters could be bathed in, inhaled, used for irrigational purposes or even drunk and were said to be '*efficace nei reumatismi, malattie cutanee, adenoidismo, asma e nelle affezioni ginecologiche*', and certainly some of the customers looked as if they might well be suffering from some or all of these complaints, which made us unwilling to join them in the pool. So whenever we visited it, and it was a fascinating place, we steeled ourselves to drink a glass of the beverage which was so horrible that we both felt that it must have been doing us good.

From the Terme a rough road led up past marble-sawing plants to the quarries at the foot of the Pizzo d'Uccello, a 1781-metre peak, otherwise known as Il Cervino dell'Apuane – the Apuan Matterhorn. Another road with something like fifteen bends in it in less than a mile led up, from Stazione Monte Bianchi at seventeen kilometres, through wild mountainous country to the mining village of Vinca, one of the loneliest in the entire massif. From it we climbed the Pizzo d'Uccello in about an hour and a half. It was worth it.

Then, at around twenty-two kilometres from Aulla, the train entered a twenty-kilometre-long tunnel and began to burrow its way under the ridge which joins the Apuan Alps to the Apennines. This ridge also forms the watershed between the Aulella, which flows westward to join the Magra at Aulla, and the Serchio, which flows down (when it flows at all) into the region known as the Garfagnana, past Lucca and then into the Ligurian Sea. From Piazza al Serchio, at a height of 494 metres the highest on the entire railway, it was downhill all the way by the river valley to Lucca, through countryside with dozens of churches hidden away in it, many of them crammed with valuable statuary, paintings and crucifixes, some of them magnificent, some since stolen, what remained of what must have been until 1944, when the Garfagnana formed part of the Gothic Line, an unimaginably rich store of religious art, all awaiting a visit from the *impresario di pompe funebri* at Fivizzano, that is if he hadn't long since already been there.

Then, after a seven-and-a-half-kilometre ride through the Lupacino Tunnel we emerged into the wide plain in which Lucca stands, where the line made a wide bend round the eastern ramparts of the city to arrive at the central station some eighty kilometres out from Fivizzano–Rometta–Soliera, what now seemed a long time ago.

⊹

What did we find after our journey through Lunigiana and the Garfagnana when the train deposited us at the central station in Piazza Ricasoli in Lucca? A walled city standing in what, up to a short time previously, when it was relentlessly built over, had been an open plain, separated from Pisa, its great rival, by a densely wooded hill, the Monte Pisano.

The principal wonders of Lucca were its walls, of which there had been three different sets. The first walls were Roman. They were about thirty feet high and the limestone employed to build them was delivered to the site hewn into cyclopean blocks. Another Roman wonder was and is an immense oval amphitheatre, built with similar blocks, and these walls were honeycombed with minute troglodytic dwellings, whose inhabitants looked down from them into the interior of the amphitheatre, which at that time housed the fruit and vegetable market.

The building of the mediaeval walls was begun in 1260. They endured until 1504 when they were razed to the ground. Work then began on the third and most complex set of walls which took 141 years to complete.

When completed they were almost three miles in circumference and consisted of eleven curtain walls, thirty-nine feet high, built with masonry and faced with six million bricks.

What about the inhabitants; what did we make of them? Well, the truth is, even after twenty-five years or so, not very much. They kept their cards close to their chests and bosoms, the Lucchesi. You would have to live among them, something I have always wanted to do, but not for ever. Nevertheless, together with Parma, Lucca remained our favourite city in Italy.

All we knew about them, the Lucchesi, was as much quoted as the piece about Petra, 'a rose-red city half as old as time', to the effect that it took twelve Jews to make a Genovese, twelve Genovesi to make a Biellese, and twelve Biellesi to make one Lucchese.

According to the presumably non-Lucchesi Italians who spread this *canard* around, it implied that they were exceptionally energetic, very able in business, cool, if not downright cold, calm, self-possessed and parsimonious. In fact as near as any of them could come to being facsimiles of Veneziani without having plastic surgery done on their noses.

However, down there for the day to have a good meal and window shop for an obelisk, which were only two of the things you could do with pleasure in Lucca, we were about as likely to encounter anyone prepared to do his or her Lucchese act for our benefit as we would be to meet up with a Scotsman counting his bawbees on the streets of Aberdeen. Probably the only way of finding out what they were really like would have been to cast ourselves into the Fossa Cunetta, the moat that surrounded the city, and see if any of them attempted to save us from drowning, that is if there was any water in it at the time.

What the Lucchesi undoubtedly were, and always had been, was square as coffee tables. They were also lovers of independence, provided that it existed within some kind of recognizable, democratic, non-egalitarian framework. Just like the Veneziani, they too were used to being members of a republic, and they too had preserved their character, or rather their multiple personalities, for similar reasons. They disliked being pushed about, and having their trade interfered with, and they were able to isolate themselves from the outside world when they needed to do so, although with walls rather than with water and raw sewage as the Veneziani had succeeded in doing.

Until the early part of the fourteenth century they had been put upon by a succession of tyrants, a few of them able, most of them nasty. In 1369 they bought their freedom from the Pisans at a cost of 100,000 florins, a transaction which, given the value of the florin at that time, and their attitude to money, must have caused them some heart-searching.

After that, apart from thirty years from 1400 to 1430 of absolute rule under Paolo Guinigi, a rich, cultivated humanist, in the course of which art and literature flourished, they maintained their republican independence.

In 1809 Napoleon gave Lucca, together with Massa Carrara, as a principality, to his sister, Elisa Baciocchi, known as the 'Semiramis of Lucca', one of whose claims to fame was that, having hastened back to Lucca when it was invested by a flood, she had herself hoisted over the walls into the city by a crane.

Down in the city, below the ramparts, in the narrow streets there were shopfronts as black and shiny as the coffins in the *pompe funebri* at Fivizzano, some of them in what Italians call *Stile Liberty* and some call *Art Nouveau*, and the Lucchesi, shopkeepers male and female, and men of business, lived much as they always had. Once they were bankers and merchants who travelled widely. Some used to traffic in woollen goods and olive oil; others in superb silks, a manufactory introduced from Sicily in the fourteenth century. These silks, many of them used for furnishing and curtains, were gorgeously dyed in blues and strawberry pinks and imperial yellows, and they were embellished with beautiful, multi-coloured ribbons which were still being woven on a set of looms in the city when we first went there, and may be still.

And there were numbers of impossibly expensive antique shops whose owners, quintessential Lucchesi, would mail you one of those aforementioned *obelischi*, or a *sarcofago*, at the drop of a traveller's cheque.

But what really kept Lucca going, and able to retain her self-assumed title as Lucca l'Industriosa, were small industries which, hidden away in the surrounding countryside, produced anything from fly-fishing rods to moccasins. Agriculture was also important. There was still a big business in fruit, wine and olive oil, the best of which was already difficult to find and was very expensive.

This was still one of the great rural centres of northern Tuscany and here, in Borgo Giannotti, a road that led to the cattle and horse markets outside the walls, you could buy articles from a pre-plastic age: wooden hay rakes, with a handle and tines that together formed part, before they were cut, of a single tree that had been grown in the form of a hay rake, forks that are still being made; big green umbrellas, made from waxed canvas with handles painted red that stained your hands for the first few years after you bought them, widely used by *contadini* working in the fields; bill hooks of all shapes and sizes; brooms, made with twigs, that looked as if they were intended to be ridden by witches, others made from the stalks of the millet, a sort which almost every Italian housewife possessed; *preti*; copper and terracotta cooking pots; chairs with rush seats, some of them for children with a trap door and a secret place underneath which concealed a *vaso da notte*.

Eventually, once it got out of the environs, Borgo Giannotti became the main road to Bagni di Lucca, known in the tenth century as Bagni di Corsena. Its springs, which contained salt and sulphur and varied in temperature between warm 39°C and downright hot 54°C, were to be found in several small villages in the valley of the Lima, a tributary of the Serchio. Back in the nineteenth century, and long before that, they enjoyed a great vogue, especially among the English, and later the Americans. Montaigne, Lamartine, Byron, Shelley, Mary Godwin, Heine and Elizabeth Browning took the waters here; but not all at once. The first recorded royal visit was that of the Holy Roman Emperor, Frederick II of Hohenstaufen in 1248 or 9, which scared the inhabitants stiff. In the 1900s there was a whole clutch of luxury hotels in Bagni di Lucca that are now no more.

And in the English cemetery (there was also an English church served by a chaplain from Pisa and an English chemist) there was the grave of Ouida, otherwise Marie Louise de la Ramé, the best-selling novelist who spent most of her working life in Florence and died in Viareggio in poverty in 1908, covered with a recumbent Carrara marble effigy of the writer with a dog at her feet. It was Ouida who was reputed to have written, when describing a race at Henley Regatta: 'All rowed fast but none rowed faster than stroke.'

After eating in Lucca, usually in a restaurant called Da Giulio in Pelleria, we used to climb up on to the ramparts and flake out in the shade on what was known as the Cérchio Arborato, the Arboreal Circle, the enfilades of great plane trees that lined them.

The view inwards over the city from the walls was more rewarding. From this dizzy height of thirty-nine feet you could look down into people's back gardens, a rather good one being the secret garden of the seventeenth-century Palazzo Pfanner, and look out over the rooftops of dozens, perhaps hundreds, of other *palazzi*, and overhead lift your eyes and look up at towers and belfries so numerous that it was rather like looking out across a forest of giant, fossilized trees. One of these towers actually had a small grove of ilex sprouting from the top of it.

However, most of the towers were those of churches; and almost all of them were difficult, if not impossible to get into because they had long since ceased to be churches, and no one knew where the keys were anyway. In fact we never met anyone who had the slightest idea how many churches there were or had been in Lucca.

The Cathedral of St Martino (sixth century) had works by Lucca's greatest sculptor, Matteo Civitali, displayed in it. One of these, his masterpiece, was an octagonal chapel, Il Tempietto, built in 1484 to house *Il Volto Santo*, the Holy Countenance, a simulacrum of Christ at Calvary by St Nicodemus, who is said to have witnessed the crucifixion.

This image, which is kept in the chapel, together with a solid gold candelabrum weighing twenty-six pounds (presented by the inhabitants in 1836, in order to avert an onset of cholera), is in fact a beautiful and very moving cedar wood crucifix of the eleventh or twelfth century, with the likeness on it, and may be a copy of an earlier one.

According to legend the image was put to sea on the shores of the Holy Land in a vessel without a crew or any means of propulsion, either oars or sails, by Guifredo, an Italian bishop, while on pilgrimage there and in 842 it grounded at Luni.

Once they discovered it the Lunesi, not unnaturally, claimed it for themselves. However, the Lucchesi, even at that early date already living up to their reputation for smartness, said that the Bishop of Lucca had already dreamt of its imminent arrival, which therefore gave Lucca a prior claim to it. And the matter was decided beyond question when the Bishop ordered two bullocks to be yoked to a driverless cart with the crucifix in it at the place where it had come ashore. This having been done, without hesitation, the animals set off for Lucca.

These miraculous happenings are remembered each year on 13 September when the procession known as La Luminara takes place. In the course of it the *Volto Santo*, clad in the *colobrium*, a long Gothic shirt worked in gold, is carried through the streets of the city which are illuminated by thousands of candles.

In some of these narrow streets in Lucca the dwellings on the ground floors were like dark caverns, in which very old ladies, also in deepest black, used to sit hour after hour making lace or crocheting, so that all one could see of them were their skeletal white hands working the whiter than white material, and their white, lined faces, like an under-exposed photograph in black and white.

Chapter Nineteen

UP TO NOW anyone reading this book may be excused for thinking that the picture I have been endeavouring to paint of our life at I Castagni is an altogether too arcadian one and the characters who have been depicted are altogether too good to be true. It was some time in the early 1970s that a cloud at first no larger than a man's hand appeared on the horizon, in reality considerably larger than a man's hand, in the form of Arturo Baldini, a farmer who was to have a baleful influence on our lives for many years to come.

He owned a property some distance up the hill from I Castagni and just like a number of other farming families, such as the Dadà, he had a number of outlying fields, one of which, a large *vigneto* he had planted some three years previously, overlooked our property on one side.

Arturo also owned the barn downhill from our house to the west which was such a fine feature in the landscape, and behind which the sun used to set so spectacularly. This was the building we had been so keen to buy in order to prevent it being knocked down at some time in the future and rebuilt as a modern house, which was a highly probable fate for it, given the sort of local authorities which held sway in these parts. At the time Signor Vescovo was negotiating the purchase of I Castagni on our behalf he told us that Arturo was adamant about not selling it, and the mere thought of trying to buy two different properties belonging to two different owners at the same time, one as indecisive as

Signor Botti and another, Signor Baldini, an unknown quantity, was quite sufficient to stop us pursuing the matter further, at least for the time being.

In fact we had already been warned by a man who chose his words extremely carefully, that Arturo was, as he put it, '*l'uomo più stupido della zona*'; but at that time we interpreted this as him being a bit slow on the uptake. It was only later that we realized that we had to deal with someone in whom gormlessness, cunning and sheer bloody-mindedness were more or less equally compounded.

At that time Arturo was about forty years old. He was married and had two grown-up children. Physically he was large and his trousers, which were supported by a wide, low-slung belt, always gave the impression that they were about to fall down.

He was an ardent Communist and whenever there was a Festa dell'Unità he and his family were always in the forefront. A Festa dell'Unità was a very mild, rustic sort of Party reunion at which no speeches ever seemed to be made and politics were hardly ever mentioned. It took place in the open air and lasted all day and far into the night, with dancing and eating and drinking. The food and drink were simple but excellent. We always thoroughly enjoyed these festivities: there was nothing sinister about them. A large part of the population still voted Communist, although how they could bring themselves to support what was by then such a run-down, ramshackle creed was a bit of a mystery. It was probably because all the other political parties in Italy were also run-down, just as ours are in Britain today, and it didn't appear to matter very much which party you voted for, or if you voted at all.

Signora Baldini was a personable, trim, young-looking woman of about the same age as her husband, and with an enigmatic smile. We normally used to see her a couple of times a day on her way down from her house to her barn and on her way back again, invariably with a basket on her head which she used to take home laden with various vegetables from a plot she cultivated.

When she made these trips the Signora followed the same

route as Arturo when he came down to his *vigneto*, either on foot or with a tractor, a track which wound down the hill from where his farmhouse was situated, no part of which was on our property at all. Up to the time when we arrived on the scene Arturo had never attempted to make use of the track past our front door, even on foot. This was the track which led from I Castagni across the torrent and up past Signora Angiolina's place to the main road where the Dadà farmhouse stood, all of which was a right-of-way, but for pedestrians only.

Once the various *esperti* had done what they had contracted to do at I Castagni, and had been paid and had taken their departure, we had more time to repose and look about us. The only one who didn't take his departure completely was Renato who always made himself available if any crisis developed connected with the fabric of the building, becoming, like Attilio, a sort of semi-permanent major-domo. It was about this time that we began to realize that Arturo was taking far more interest in our affairs than our brief acquaintanceship with him seemed to warrant; and this eventually became just one source of what were to be a number of minor and not-so-minor irritations.

For instance, what became one of his principal pleasures, which he took care not to indulge in when his wife was around, was to stand on the highest point in his *vigneto*, a rural version of Stout Cortez on a peak in Darien, and look down into one of our fields, which was out of sight from any other quarter, which was the reason why we used it for sunbathing.

Reclining in it, anointed with insect repellent, we took particular care not to expose ourselves completely. We both wore shorts and kept shirts handy so that we could put them on quickly if we heard anyone coming down the hill to visit us. We both knew, from long experience, that *contadini*, especially older ones, had a real horror of nakedness; to such an extent that, according to Wanda, who had female informants, many male *contadini* had never seen their wives unclothed, even in bed.

And if we had been in any doubt about this it was Signora Angiolina who, when speaking of a friend of hers who had had her first sight of a bikini, said to Wanda, as if unfolding some incredible secret, 'You know, Signora Wanda, that there are women and girls at Bocca di Magra who bathe in the sea and wear nothing but *mutande e reggiseni* [knickers and bras].' And we ourselves had once seen at Sistiana, near Trieste, a whole coachload of female *contadini* from the interior of Slovenia disporting themselves in the sea with all their clothes on.

But Arturo was not really interested in observing the Newbys lounging around in shorts, although he still continued to get some sensation from keeping an eye on Wanda if he could only surprise her shirtless. What he really enjoyed, and took advantage of whenever the opportunity presented itself, was to look down on our female guests, friends of my daughter mostly, one or two of whom, in spite of our imploring them not to do so, persisted in lying about in the most minimal bikinis in what were highly provocative postures.

Eventually, to save what remained of our reputations in the locality, we were forced to put an absolute prohibition on the wearing of bikinis in this field, or anywhere else at I Castagni, after it filtered back to us that Arturo, who in this case was not entirely to blame, had been heard to say, having seen a girl of truly amazing proportions wobbling around in the field, '*Darei uno dei miei campi per un culo come quello!*' ('I would give one of my fields for an arse like that!'). Although what he would have done with it, other than frame it, was not clear.

Arturo also had an artistic side to his nature which manifested itself on one occasion when, uninvited, he came down from his perch in his *vigneto* and stood immediately behind a distinguished artist who had come to paint at I Castagni, craning over the unfortunate man's shoulder, where he sat at his easel, gazing at the canvas and uttering a series of sounds that bore an unfortunate resemblance to derisive laughter.

One autumn, Wanda gave an enormous dinner for all our neighbours, among them the Baldinis, whom we invited only after considerable heart-searchings, although the Signora could not be blamed for her husband's voyeuristic tendencies.

I, rather stupidly, was at some pains to buy some 'good wine' for the occasion from one of the expensive shops in Sarzana. When the evening of the dinner came, which was a great success with fourteen people sitting down to eat it, including Attilio, almost everyone brought their own wine with them, ostensibly as a gift, but really because he or she would only drink local wine made by themselves or their neighbours. They all refused to drink the labelled wines from Sarzana on the grounds that they were almost certainly *lavorati*, mucked about with, which was almost certainly true. Eventually, with some misgivings, I produced our own wine which they all said was *buono*.

The following morning, while we were still clearing up from the night before, Arturo arrived at the house and without referring to the previous evening said, without any other preamble, and in a hectoring manner, that from now on he was going to use the footpath in front of our house as a *diritto di passaggio*, a right-of-way for agricultural vehicles and instruments, which could be tractors, bulldozers, trailers, ploughs, harrows and anything else he could think of. One of the vehicles he said airily he might well want to use was something called a *furgoncino*, a sort of three-wheeled delivery van, although he didn't actually own one. And he said he would go to law to enforce his right.

We were taken completely by surprise by all this, and we told him he only had the right, as did everyone else, to pass in front of the house on foot, and if we allowed him to do what he asked a general right-of-way would be created which, up to now, had never existed. How, we asked him, could anyone have used the bread oven which was built at least a hundred years ago, at the same time as the house, if wheeled traffic had been permitted to use the path, at this point only a few feet wide. If he drove his vehicles in front of our kitchen door they would run bang through the middle of our al fresco dining room.

He said that there had always been a general right-of-way and that it was he who had employed a bulldozer driver to help repair the bridge over the torrent so that it could once again support agricultural machines.

'What do you do now when you want to drive your tractor from your house to your barn and up again?' we asked him, knowing that up to now he had always used the other track, but he didn't answer.

We then offered to let him use the way round the back of the house, as a favour, which was a pretty silly thing to do, but fortunately it didn't sink in.

'He's mad to go to law,' Wanda said, 'but that's no consolation. We'll be dam' lucky if we aren't ruined. In Italy a thing like this can go on for ever.'

The following day Arturo appeared with a cow on a length of rope and in order to give it room to pass picked up our dining table and plonked it down outside our bathroom door. He then waited for the animal to produce an enormous cow flop on the paving stones.

By now we ourselves were both pretty angry, and so was he; and we told him to go back to where he came from, which he did, rather surprisingly, leaving us this steaming cow flop as a memento of his visit. Whether a cow was a *mezzo agricolo* was not clear.

That day we went down to consult Signor Vescovo as to what we should do. He said that Arturo had no such right-of-way, and neither had anyone else, and that we should get ourselves a lawyer. In the meantime we should drive a couple of poles into the ground near the torrent, suspend a chain across the track and put up a notice to the effect that this was *Proprietà Privata: Soltanto Passaggio Pedonale*, Private Property: Pedestrians Only – but still allowing enough room for people to pass on foot.

Having done this we set off for Sarzana to find ourselves a lawyer, one that Signor Vescovo had recommended to us; but when we eventually ran him to ground we discovered that he was a criminal lawyer who might be of use to us in the future if we actually did away with Arturo, something which I often contemplated doing during the ensuing years (by pushing him down our well – the water wasn't drinkable anyway); but was not what we wanted at the moment.

Fortunately, we were able to find a civil lawyer and after we had explained our predicament to him he agreed to take us on.

That same afternoon, when we got back to the house from Sarzana we found that someone, presumably Arturo, had taken the chain down (there were no padlocks), pulled up the poles and chucked the *Proprietà Privata: Soltanto Passaggio Pedonale* notices into the torrent.

The following day we received a letter from Arturo's lawyer enclosing an order signed by a judge, ordering us to remove the obstruction we had put up immediately and that Arturo had the right to pass with *mezzi agricoli*. This for us was a shattering pronouncement.

The next day our *avvocato* came to see us. The weather was appalling, the sort of *scirocco* weather we had the day we bought the house when it poured all the time; but Wanda gave us a lovely lunch with lots of *vino*. He was a nice humorous man and later, while I was showing him the boundaries of our two properties, Arturo found us standing under a couple of umbrellas peeing against one of his olive trees and roaring with laughter, which upset him. It wasn't really very much of a satisfaction, upsetting him; we seemed to be in the soup. Our lawyer told us to take photographs of Arturo using his own track for the passage of agricultural vehicles, and also to keep a journal giving a blow-by-blow account of the various humiliations he would undoubtedly heap on us before we could stop him. He also said that cases such as this one could drag on indefinitely because, judicially and monetarily speaking, they were unimportant and no one could be bothered to bring them to a conclusion. He was only too right. In fact, the length of time this one dragged on for exceeded everyone's wildest expectations.

That year the rest of the so-called holiday in Italy was a nightmare, and so were many succeeding ones, with Arturo passing in front of our house with his tractor dragging agricultural instruments, trailers full of manure, *bigonci* and sometimes jeering members of his clan, the tractor smashing the flagstones on which our table stood, which he always removed and never replaced. On one occasion he actually picked up the table while we were eating our midday meal at it. All we could do was inform our lawyer of the latest developments and keep the bloody diary. But we got bored with it after a year or so and gave it up. Meanwhile Arturo and his wife always used the other route to go down to their property and back on foot, as the distance was much shorter.

'*Et in Arcadia ego,*' was what Wanda said on one occasion when we were being further humiliated, practically blind with rage.

Years later, neither of us can now remember how many, a meeting took place at I Castagni at which were present the protagonists – the Newbys and Baldinis, a Sicilian judge, the two opposing lawyers and an impressive number of witnesses, those on Arturo's side all testifying that the right-of-way in front of our house had always been open to agricultural vehicles, and this was the only way Arturo could get from his farmyard to his barn. Our lawyer chose this moment to produce the photographs we had taken of Arturo driving his tractor with a loaded trailer in tow up the other track. At the same time all the Dadà and Signora Angiolina testified to the fact that Arturo was not telling the truth when he said that the road down to our house had been bulldozed years ago by a man named Baretti who was from the Canis' village, Castelnovo ne' Monti. By this time it was obvious that the judge was not pleased at having such small fry attempting to pull the wool over his eyes, after having been used to dealing with rather more imposing characters in his native island, and we felt we had scored a small but important point and that far away on the horizon there was a glimmer of hope, but one much smaller than a man's hand.

The following day Wanda drove to Castelnovo ne' Monti. There she tracked down Signor Baretti, the driver of the bulldozer, who told her that he had only worked with it on the main road to Fosdinovo and had never set eyes on our house or the torrent in the whole of his life; and he said that he was willing to testify in Sarzana to this effect, providing someone paid his fare. We had to wait seven years before we could call him and it was lucky for us that after so long he was still alive.

Arturo's rather unstrict regard for the truth even brought down a condemnation from Attilio. He made a pronouncement, *urbi et orbi*, to the effect that if this right-of-way for agricultural vehicles existed, and Arturo knew about it, and the owner of the house, Signor Botti, knew about it, which he didn't, why didn't he, Attilio, know about it. After which he withdrew into one of his innumerable shells. Signor Botti then testified in a rather quavering voice, due solely to age rather than awe of the judiciary, that there never had been any such right-of-way.

One would have thought that Signor Botti's testimony would have been enough to sink the opposition and bring the matter to a speedy conclusion but this was Italy where, at that time, the law was in a similar state of demoralization as it is in Britain today.

✝

The next confrontation took place in the Tribunale, the Law Courts at Sarzana. Present at this meeting was another judge, the Sicilian having died from natural causes since our last coming together up the hill – a pity, we had rather liked him – and the two opposing lawyers. Present also were those witnesses who had not yet sunk into the tomb, or been so discredited that they were of no further use. Witnesses of any sort were becoming a bit thin on the ground. As we were setting off to drive to Sarzana for this meeting we were asked by a Signor Lazzari if we would give him a lift down to the Tribunale as otherwise he would be late for the proceedings. He and his wife had been among the guests at Wanda's dinner party and up to this time we had always helped them with their *vendemmia*. It was only when we got to the Tribunale that we found out that the reason why he had been in such a hurry was because he was going to act as a witness on Arturo's behalf.

This was the meeting, when Signor Lazzari had just finished testifying that a road across the torrent had been bulldozed by Signor Baretti, that Wanda's star witness from Castelnovo ne' Monti, Signor Baretti himself, was produced and any chance of Arturo winning this terrible case was finally extinguished.

After this it would not have been unreasonable to hope for a speedy conclusion to this Dickensian, Dodson and Fogg kind of litigation: but although judgement was promised, and there was very little doubt about what the outcome would be, more years were to pass before it was actually handed down, in spite of the efforts of our lawyer who, with the passage of all these years, had become an old friend.

What was intolerable was that, without a judgement being handed down, Arturo still continued to exercise his right-of-way through our property.

Eventually, when we were in the depths of despair about *La Causa*, which was the Kafkaesque name by which we had come to know it, judgement was given against Arturo who had to pay all the costs of an affair which had taken fifteen years to resolve. We did not feel like celebrating what was a Pyrrhic victory if ever there was one.

A short time later Arturo died and it was not until then that we discovered the reason why he had been so keen on acquiring the right-of-way. Apparently, he had had the intention of getting permission to knock down his barn and build a house which would require a right-of-way to get to it. Arturo's own right-of-way included a section which was not his property and the owner of it was not prepared to cede the right-of-way to him. And there was no other route available to him.

Eventually, the barn was converted into a house and the whole business of the right-of-way showed signs of starting up again; but by that time we no longer owned I Castagni. So passed Arturo.

Chapter Twenty

IT WAS ONE SPRING, the day after we arrived at I Castagni from England, that Signora Dadà died. She was the wife of Signor Settimo Dadà, the ex-member of the Alpini who had fought in the First World War. It was he who, together with Attilio, had set up the *pergola* outside our house which now, with wild vines proliferating over it at a tremendous rate, provided us with blessed shade when we ate outdoors. Trying to separate one lot of Dadà from another was like being in a hall of mirrors.

The Signora died at the age of eighty-six after a long illness. And when we asked Signora Angiolina what would be the most appropriate way to pay our respects to her – this was the first death of anyone in the neighbourhood with whom we were acquainted – she said that our presence would be much appreciated at the *veglia funebre*, the vigil or wake, that would take place that evening, the night before the funeral, and would last the entire night, to '*benedire la defunta*', to ask God's favour for the dead woman, was how she put it.

It was quite dark and beginning to rain when we crossed the torrent which separated our property from that of Signor Settimo and went up towards his house by a succession of steep, winding paths through a series of minute fields, most of which were planted with vines and vegetables. Tonight the light in the yard had been turned on to guide any mourners to it who were coming to pay their respects and it was now visible as a blur in the general murk overhead.

When we finally reached the house and gained admission it was so full of people that it looked as if it was about to burst at the seams. Besides Signor Settimo, Signora Maria, Signor Settimo's eldest daughter, who was married to Signor Orfeo, the one who had been in Russia with the Alpini in the Second World War, there was Signora Anna, Signor Settimo's youngest daughter, and large numbers of relatives and close friends; and as a very wetting rain was now falling no one wanted to be left outside.

This was the first *veglia* I had ever attended, whereas Wanda had been to many, and although of course I didn't know it at the time, it was to be an almost uncanny facsimile of those that took place when, some time later, a contemporary of Wanda's mother, in Slovene Nunča Pahorča, pronounced Nunsa Pahuzza (Nunča in English being Aunt), died in what was an Italian part of the Carso – the limestone country inland from the Adriatic – at the age of ninety-three. And it was more or less identical, apart from the singing, which was much better in the Carso than here in Italy, with my own mother-in-law's *bedenje*, the Slovene equivalent to a *veglia*, when she died at the same age, some years after that.

The signora, dressed in deepest black, from black lace *velo* to black felt slippers, was laid out in an upstairs bedroom in a black wooden coffin of the sort that was still being turned out on the production line in the *pompe funebri* at Fivizzano. She lay in it on her own linen sheets, part of her dowry some sixty years previously which she had kept unused in a bottom drawer ready for this particular eventuality; in her crossed hands a rosary, her features waxen white, like those of the lace-makers at Lucca.

At each of the four corners of the bed on which the coffin stood, a tall candle was burning, and at the foot of it there were sprigs of box and a receptacle containing holy water. Around the walls, sitting on benches and chairs, a tight fit, were a number of women, old and young, and a few elderly men, one of whom, wearing a black tie, was Attilio. The women were reciting the rosary and, when they had finished, they talked about the deceased and her virtues and good things they remembered about her, some of which were funny and made them laugh. And from time to time they had a little drink of good white wine. And this they would continue to do, in relays, for a great part of the night.

And now, to pay our respects, we each took a sprig of box and dipped it in the holy water and sprinkled it over the corpse, and then after a bit we went downstairs to clasp the hands of the bereaved and have a drink from a bottle of Scotch malt whisky which Signor Orfeo had bought in Sarzana for the purpose.

The following morning, which was cold and clear, the coffin containing the body of Signora Dadà was carried up to the road from the house by a party of four men who were either relatives or friends, and there it was loaded into the van, all that the Municipio of Fosdinovo seemed able or willing to offer for the funeral of a lady of modest circumstances.

Modest or not there were a lot of people ready and waiting to take part in the procession up to Fosdinovo where the funeral service was to take place. The men were all wearing black ties and many of them were dressed in black, as were the majority of the women. Almost everyone we knew around I Castagni was there, including Attilio, and as soon as the coffin was loaded into the makeshift hearse everyone fell in behind it. The priest who was leading the procession was the good-looking young man whom we had never seen before who had succeeded the old one with whom we had careered round the ramparts on our first Good Friday at Fosdinovo, and who had recently retired.

Now, flanked by a couple of acolytes who had been given special leave of absence from their school down at Caniparola so that they could perform their functions, he took up his station in front of the hearse and gave the signal to advance.

And now we were off with the van, which seemed to have a wonky clutch and to be on its last legs, juddering up the hill in first gear, and behind it, stretching away down the hill and around one of the hairpin bends, the column of mourners, like a long, black, undulating snake.

About half-way up the hill from I Castagni to Fosdinovo the van gave a final shudder and conked out completely, emitting a strong smell of burnt clutch. It was a grotesque thing to happen on what was otherwise a dignified, solemn and moving occasion, although it was difficult to expunge the memory of another disastrous rural funeral in the film *Monsieur Hulot's Holiday*.

But no further grotesque happenings were allowed to mar the occasion and the four men who had carried the coffin from the house to the hearse now slid it out of the vehicle, lifted it on their shoulders, and carried it up the last half-mile or so to the Church of San Remigio, with the women reciting the rosary and the men the *Requiem Aeternam*, in low, rumbling voices that sounded like distant thunder:

> *dona eis Domine*
> *et lux perpetua*
> *luceat eis . . .*

Up through what had been the Porta Genovese, the lower of the two gates of the town before it was destroyed in the last war; up past the signora's hotel and the butcher's shop and the Oratorio dei Bianchi, from which we had set out with Attilio; and up to San Remigio with a big bell tolling overhead, the number of those taking part in the procession increasing all the way to it.

There in the church the young priest conducted the service in a manner which everyone agreed was both *solenne e familiare*.

After this the final journey began: with the priest and his acolytes still out ahead of the coffin which by now had a new band of bearers – as a hernia-less male I had rather expected to be recruited into it myself; then up through the town, along the foot of the walls of the Castello and out through what is known as the Porta Fiorentina, the main gate, so called, rather confusingly, because it actually led out to the road that eventually took you, not to Florence but to Fivizzano, which was originally in Florentine territory, hence the name. We then crossed a causeway to the junction of three roads: the road from Caniparola, the one leading to the Foce il Cuccù and Fivizzano, and the Strada della Spoverina which wound its way from Fosdinovo through the steep, densely wooded foothills of the Apuan Alps to Carrara.

Near the meeting place of the three roads was the cemetery and there, after a brief service of committal, the remains of the signora were finally laid to rest in one of a series of what looked like giant marble filing cabinets which enclosed the cemetery and which had other parallel avenues of them leading off on either side. In them every occupant had his or her allotted space, the length and breadth of a coffin, one above the other and cheek by jowl, and into one of these the bearers now slid the coffin containing the signora. And so that there could be no confusion, the details of who was in a particular file were carved on the marble door in black lettering and a photograph depicting the deceased was reproduced on a porcelain plaque.

And there she was left with the flowers and a little oil lamp that would burn as long as anyone who knew her was left alive to keep it alight. And that night there would be hundreds of these little lights burning in the cemetery to keep her company.

Although none of us knew it at the time this funeral was an historic event. It was the last time that a procession on foot would accompany a coffin up to Fosdinovo. From now on, if anyone died, those who followed behind the hearse did so by car.

✝

The following week the priest came down the hill and blessed all the houses and their occupants, including I Castagni, which was the custom once a year. Afterwards he always stayed on to have a drink and a chat. This, he said when we first met him, was his first command as a parish priest but although he had been full of trepidation about how he would be received, everyone had been very kind to him. The only thing that was really troubling him was not important but he intensely disliked the cold blue-grey colour of the interior of his church, San Remigio, which he described as *molto triste*, a judgement with which we were both inclined to agree.

However, he went on, when it came to choosing another, warmer colour, although the funds were available for what was a badly needed re-painting whatever colour was chosen, various factions declared themselves, each of which had a different colour scheme in mind, and this did not take into consideration the quite large number of his parishioners who liked the colour it was painted and appeared to be ready to fight to the death against any re-painting at all unless it was carried out in the same shade. Subsequently, it was Kenneth Rowntree, the painter who had attracted the derisive laughter of Arturo, and his wife, Diana, who devised a colour scheme for the church at Fosdinovo which delighted the priest and satisfied everyone else.

Chapter Twenty-One

FROM TIME TO TIME when we were staying at I Castagni we used to make excursions into the wild country that was little known to foreigners, high up on the Tuscan side of the Apennines. There we found villages, some of which had been partly or completely abandoned by their inhabitants. In them there was abundant evidence of a way of life, what archaeologists would probably quite soon be referring to as the *civiltà contadina*, a way of life that, apart from a few practitioners of it such as Attilio, Signor Anselmo who was still dropping in on us for a drink on his way to have his hair cut, Signor Settimo, the old Alpino, and the husband of Signora Zaira, the lady who kept a black cow, whose name I have forgotten, would soon be extinct.

One of the largest of these villages, one which we had always wanted to visit although it was by no means abandoned, or even partially so, was Sassalbo which was hidden away below the main road from Fivizzano to Reggio Emilia, which crosses the Apennines at the Passo del Ceretto.

When we finally decided to go we also invited Signor Giuseppe, Signora Fernanda and Signora Angiolina to come with us as none of them, so far as we could make out, had ever been much further into the outside world than the Sarzana market.

Their first reactions to our invitation were not quite as enthusiastic as we had hoped they would be. Apparently the Sassalbini were no strangers so far as they were concerned and they viewed the opportunity of renewing their acquaintanceship with them with a certain amount of misgiving. According to them the Sassalbini used to travel all over Lunigiana, and even further afield, going from door to door selling the *pecorino* cheeses for which they were renowned, and to some extent they still did so. They had a reputation in northern Tuscany for being as hard as nails. There was even an old saying, which Signora Angiolina now proceeded to quote with relish, to the effect that, '*quando incontri un Sassalbino lascialo andare per il suo cammino*' ('when you meet a Sassalbino let him go his own way').

Nevertheless, in spite of all this, the thought of going for a day out more or less extinguished their prejudices against visiting a place that for them, together with its inhabitants, had some of the characteristics that parts of Africa still have for me.

It was left to Signor Giuseppe to put a further damper on the plan when he decreed that Signora Fernanda would have to stay behind to guard their two houses, in case a band of robbers descended on them like locusts and stripped them of their contents.

It was unfortunate that the choice for this boring and quite unnecessary chore fell on Signora Fernanda, who was really looking forward to going on this excursion, rather than on Signora Angiolina, because Signora Angiolina was not considered by Signor Giuseppe to be sufficiently robust to repel robbers. She herself wasn't really all that keen on going to Sassalbo because she was worried about what would happen to her rabbits in her absence. However, when Signora Fernanda heard that she had been chosen to remain behind, she put on a brave face and prepared a substantial *merenda* for the four of us.

The village was partly hidden in a large grove of chestnuts, some of which had attained an enormous size. It stood at the foot of the cliffs below the Passo Cerreto on the right bank of a torrent called the Rosaro which had its origins just below the main ridge of the Apennines which loomed high overhead. When it was in flood, as it often was after a storm, the Rosaro brought down huge quantities of rocks and gravel leaving a stony, bone-dry wasteland in its path when it eventually subsided. At that time, before the road down to it was improved, Sassalbo was really remote, in winter often cut off from the outside world for long periods of time. And that morning, with its rather grim, grey stone houses which were roofed with heavy slabs of the same material, and its cowsheds which were made to match them, from which came the lowing sounds of cattle, it really did have a feeling of being a place at the world's end.

At this moment its cobbled lanes were crowded with mules which had been bringing firewood down into the village from somewhere higher up the mountainside, and they were now being unloaded by their drivers, a bunch of hard-looking men, of a sort that I, personally, would not have been altogether happy about purchasing cheese from, whether *pecorino* or any other sort.

Apart from these muleteers, most of the inhabitants of Sassalbo that morning appeared to be women – the children were at school – all of them wearing hand-knitted woollen stockings and mountain boots; while a surprising number of them, even quite young ones, were dressed in deep mourning.

Until the outbreak of the Second World War the population of Sassalbo had numbered about 1500 persons. Fourteen men had been killed in the First World War, twenty in the Second. By the late 1940s or early 1950s, the population was 917. Up to that time the Sassalbini had owned big flocks of sheep and they had made a not-very-good living selling their *pecorino* cheese. It was then that the men of Sassalbo began to leave their village, as did the men who left hundreds and thousands of other villages in search of work in the cities, in France, Germany and many other parts of western Europe. From then onwards Sassalbo became virtually a village of women and children, except at certain times of year such as August, Christmas and Easter when most of the men who could afford to do so came home.

The women augmented their earnings by spinning wool, gathering chestnuts and milking their cows. They were a strange, withdrawn sort of people but given their remote situation it was scarcely surprising. There were still, when we went there, a number of shepherds around Sassalbo, each of whom had a flock of about three hundred sheep. They took them up to the *crinale* around 20 June, together with their dogs, and usually stayed there with them, living in their huts and sleeping on beds made with beech boughs until October, when the weather began to break. They then took the flocks down in lorries to the Maremma, the fertile area near the shores of the Tyrrhenian Sea, where they passed the winter, the shepherds renting whatever pasture they needed for the animals. Until after the last war they used to drive the sheep down to the Maremma on foot; but now the volume of traffic on the roads made this impossible.

Down by the river the sheep were being sheared in great numbers and the air was filled with their lamentations. The shepherds, men in their late twenties, were using hand-forged shears. Mist began to sweep down the screes from the *passo*, and suddenly Sassalbo was a cold place to be in.

Milk with which the *pecorino* cheese was made was now the only worthwhile commodity the sheep produced, so far as making a profit was concerned, the shepherds said, while resting between shearing sheep which was tough work with primitive hand shears. Their fathers had been shepherds before them, and now they perceived themselves to be in a sort of trap with no real future to look forward to.

Few people wanted the wool any more – this was in the late 1960s and early 1970s; but until recently, the vests and socks worn by all the country people had been made from it. It was still on sale in some market places, but very few people now bought it. The wool was too rough for modern tastes. Soon, they said, they would be shearing the sheep and throwing away the wool.

This was the wool the women used to spin while watching over the flocks, or when walking from one place to another, or when sitting by the fire, or simply while talking to a neighbour. Each one carried a wooden spindle tapered at either end, with a perforated stone in the middle of it, at the top of which the woollen yarn they were spinning was attached, with the rest of the wool wound round a distaff, a piece of wood which was carried tucked under one arm.

In the *caffè* in Sassalbo four old men were playing *briscola*, smashing their cards down on the table as if they were trying to split it in two, swearing dreadful religious oaths of the kind known as *bestemmie* (the only words they uttered that I could understand), and contesting every point as if they were temperamental tennis players at Wimbledon. Or else discussing what sounded as if it might be some ancient wrong – probably, as Wanda said, something connected with a right-of-way.

During a lull in what sounded remarkably like a battle, while one of the players went off to the lavatory, Wanda took the opportunity to ask one of the remaining players, an authoritative-looking man, if he knew anyone who had any old furniture to sell.

This brought on a dead silence while the other two players watched the one to whom the question had been addressed, as if awaiting the pronouncement of an oracle. By this time, the fourth man had returned and he, too, had to be put in the picture which took some minutes. What emerged eventually from the mouth of the man who had been asked the question in the first place was a collection of sounds of a similar sort to those we had already been listening to, presumably in the Sassalbino dialect. It seemed unlikely that all four of them could have been suffering from a speech defect.

Apparently somebody's cousin had a very fine old *madia* that she might be persuaded to part with, providing the price was right. 'But you understand, Signora, that this is a very valuable piece. Would she like to give it a glance?' All this was translated for her benefit by Signor Giuseppe who appeared to be able to understand the *dialetto Sassalbino*.

And Wanda, although she didn't need a *madia*, as she already had one, said yes. So the *briscola* player's little nephew was dispatched with the four of us behind him in Indian file down the narrow alleys to visit the place where the *madia* was on view, which turned out to be a small shop selling a bit of everything.

The *madia* could be seen through the back door of the shop, standing in a yard where it obviously had been for some time as one of its front legs had moss growing on it, and the whole thing had been painted a horrible shade of green which didn't quite go with the moss. Closer examination showed that after being painted it had become infested with woodworm and it now gave the impression that it might well turn to powder if it was moved.

We all looked at it for some time, during which Signora Angiolina said, '*Ma!*' very audibly and Signor Giuseppe began humming one of the tunes he used to hum when coming down the hill to I Castagni, and wanted to warn us of his imminent arrival on the premises.

'How much are you asking for this?' Wanda asked the cousin of someone or other who, although only about twenty, was already dressed in the fashionable black, had a wedding ring on her finger, and looked like the Miss Otis of Sassalbo.

'*Quanto costa?*'

'You know,' the cousin said in a voice that had very little *dialetto* of any kind in it, but had probably been developed in the sixth form at Fivizzano High, 'that this is a piece that is extremely valuable.'

'*Quanto?*' said Wanda.

'I couldn't consider selling it,' the cousin said, very seriously, 'for less than forty thousand lire. It has been in our family, here at Sassalbo, for many, many years.'

'I cannot buy your *madia*,' Wanda said. 'I suggest you should continue to keep it in your family.'

'*E una ladra*,' ('She's a thief,') Signor Giuseppe said when we were once more out in the lane, on the cobbles. He sounded really happy. His worst forebodings about the Sassalbini had been more than realized.

He was even more happy when the parish priest, having been apprised of our arrival on some papal grapevine, had sent an emissary to the *caffè* to invite us to view what he described as a fine old *letto matrimoniale*, which he no longer had any need for. What a priest was doing with a double bed in the first place was not clear. Basically it was quite a good metal bed for two people, but its mother-of-pearl embellishments, and the little pastoral scenes which should have appeared in oval frames at either end, had all been painted over. In fact the whole bed had been painted with something that smelt like tar. Why it had been treated in this barbarous manner was a mystery.

His estimate of the value of this now hideous object was fifty thousand lire. None of us really believed that he was going, as he said, to devote the proceeds of the sale to the improvement of the church.

'*Anche lui é un ladro,*' ('He's also a thief,') Signor Giuseppe said happily. It reinforced his feelings, as a supporter of the Left, about the Italian clergy in general.

And now we drove away, still further into the mountains, from this strange, rather sad village, the like of which, we all agreed, none of us had ever seen.

✛

Almost twenty-five years were to elapse before we visited Sassalbo again. By the time we did, the year before we left I Castagni, Sassalbo had changed not beyond recognition but sufficiently to make one rub one's eyes. It was not only the village that had changed, the inhabitants also had undergone a degree of metamorphosis. Many of the old houses had been rendered with cement and only very few had the big stone flags we remembered on the roofs. Most of them now had red tiles and inside many of them were equipped with modern kitchens, baths and bidets. Outside most of the cobbled lanes had been cemented over. All this prosperity was paid for by those expatriate Sassalbini, some of whom had returned to Sassalbo to pass the evening of their days; others still working abroad, those whose Peugeots, Renaults, Mercedes and Toyotas now filled the lanes at holiday times. The day we were there the funeral took place of a man aged eighty-five, bringing the population down from 150 to 149. And now in the entire village there was only one cow.

But there were still shepherds who had big flocks of sheep; and the shepherds still sold the cheese, but nobody sold the wool any more; and no one spun it; and very few people wore black; and the place was full of teenagers, mostly students. In fact it was all much more *allegro* than it had ever been.

Chapter Twenty-Two

A S THE YEARS PASSED death claimed many of the people in the countryside round about I Castagni whom we had got to know so well.

The first to die, of what country people always call *un brutto male* (it was never called cancer), after a long and painful illness, was Signor Dadà Modesto, Signora Maria's husband, a loss she bore with a stoicism which one would have expected of her. Her elder son, Tranquillo, then became head of the family and Rina assumed her mother-in-law's role in the hierarchy of this *famiglia reale*.

When his father died, Valentino, Tranquillo's younger brother, returned to Italy from the Middle East where he had been working for an English engineering firm, and subsequently he married Gloria, a good-looking, intelligent local schoolmistress with a will of her own. Valentino then acquired an agency for the sale and servicing of tractors and bulldozers in the area. They had a daughter called Francesca.

Meanwhile Tranquillo's eldest son, Paolo, who had come to stay with us in Devon – at that time he was still a schoolboy and was much impressed by the treelessness of Dartmoor, the mist and the prison – married Doriana, a lively red-headed girl. They opened a food shop in Fosdinovo but people were already beginning to desert their village shops, preferring to travel to Sarzana where there was a bigger selection and lower prices, and their venture failed. Subsequently an enormous *supermercato* opened at Ponte Isolone and a number of other small businesses failed too.

Meanwhile, with the aid of their parents, Paolo and Doriana had built a house on the way down from I Castagni to Caniparola where the shops and the Communist cell were. There, as the Cani boys had done, he acquired a tractor and hired it out with himself as driver, and with this he was more successful. They, too, had a daughter.

Paolo's younger brother, Michele, had the great misfortune, soon after leaving school, to damage one of his eyes very seriously when a splinter of metal entered it while he was welding and, in spite of being taken by his parents to see two of the foremost eye specialists, one in Spain, the other in Britain, neither of them was able to save it.

The next to die was Signor Dadà Settimo. His son-in-law, Signor Orfeo, became head of the family, and soon afterwards retired on pension from the dockyard at La Spezia to cultivate his piece of land.

After him it was Signor Cani, one of the so-called foreigners who came originally from Castelnovo ne' Monti, the father of Alice who made dresses for Wanda, and of her two brothers, the ones who drove tractors.

Another who died was the husband of Signora Zaira, herself the last in the neighbourhood to keep a cow. They lived in one of the picturesque but primitive Malaspina houses, the sort with a plaque on its façade stating which Malaspina had erected it and when. He was a blacksmith but when the demand for handmade agricultural instruments such as spades and forks declined, he went over to making ladders. He also made clogs and he had been the last to make sledges, for which there was no demand any more. Signora Zaira loved her cow and she used to make wonderful cakes using the cream from the milk.

The next to die was Signor Bergamaschi, the plumber, who installed our Velodoccia, the one he blew a hole in.

And then, at long last, someone we hardly dared to think of dying, because she was so much a part of our lives, Signora

Angiolina. She also had the *brutto male* and her sister Signora Fernanda and her brother-in-law Signor Giuseppe took her in to their house and she slept, that is when she slept at all, on a couch in their best room. She was very brave and when the time came for us to return to England she told us that if anything happened to her we were not to come; and that she would always think of us with love, and that the times when we had been at I Castagni were amongst the happiest of her life.

When she died, although Signora Fernanda had promised to let us know, she didn't do so because Signora Angiolina had begged her not to, and it was not until a week after she was dead and buried that Signora Fernanda sent us the news. It was good to know that Attilio had represented us at the funeral.

As a result of this Silvano, the son of Signor Giuseppe and Signora Fernanda, together with his wife and young daughter came to live up the hill and built a house next door to them. Silvano could do anything from re-wiring a house to making shoes, both skills that he had learned professionally.

The cruellest losses of all were reserved for Renato. His wife suffered a difficult death, also from the *brutto male*. His daughter, Fiorella, who at that time must have been about sixteen, volunteered to go down on her motor scooter, to collect a further supply of morphia for her mother from a chemist's shop, and was run down and killed on the Via Aurelia by a drunken lorry driver, who was never sent to trial. Her mother died a week or two later.

Renato was a survivor. There was no doubt about that. He had survived the SS massacre at San Terenzo and now he survived the deaths of his wife and daughter; but neither of us dared to think of what went on in his heart. It was at this time, too, that another of our near neighbours died of Alzheimer's disease.

Another casualty, again a fatal one, was the young priest whom everyone liked so much who had come to bless our house and had worked so hard to cheer up the interior of his church at Fosdinovo. He fell in love with a girl who was a schoolmistress and was excommunicated and forced to leave the priesthood.

They were subsequently married and had a child, and then, he was never very strong, he died.

☩

And then we lost Attilio. One spring he began to complain of pains in his stomach – *'non mi sento molto bene'* ('I don't feel very well') was about all we could get out of him – and when the local doctor was consulted he gave Attilio a letter to take to the hospital at Carrara. When we arrived there with him he was admitted as suffering from some complaint of the kidneys, which was causing them to fail. Apparently it was not possible to operate.

Sitting up in his hospital bed, dressed in a white nightshirt, for the first time we were seeing him without his cap, he looked like a schoolboy in a dormitory, and chattered away like one. Every time we came to see him he was very pleased, especially to see Wanda, *'la mia padrona'*.

By now he was getting thinner and thinner and more quiet, and then one evening he simply faded away. One moment he was there, the next he was gone, just as he had so often been in life, just as he disappeared outside the Church of San Remigio on that first Good Friday that now seemed, and was, so long ago.

☩

And as these *contadini* we had known so well departed this life, so the little world they had inhabited also began to die and was supplanted by one that would have been difficult for them to comprehend, as difficult as it was for those who survived them, such as ourselves. This radical change in their way of life began to become apparent about the time when, long after the death of Signor Modesto, the Dadà demolished their old farmhouse and built a new one on the same site.

It was far more comfortable than the old farmhouse. They divided this new one into two separate apartments on the upper floor, with balconies that gave a magnificent view of the Magra and the sea. One was for Tranquillo and his family, the other for Valentino and his, each with a bathroom and separate kitchens. Meanwhile Signora Maria still continued to use the original kitchen and her bedroom on the ground floor that had been incorporated in the new building. This led, inevitably, to the family becoming more dispersed (Paolo and his wife already had their own house down the hill) and it became much more rare to see them *en masse*, although on some days of *festa* we still made excursions with Tranquillo and Rina to other parts of Tuscany, and also had midday and evening meals on Sundays with them, either in Tranquillo's or Valentino's place where the entire family assembled for the event.

It was at this time that Rina gave up milking her cow, Bionda, as, soon after, did Signora Zaira down the hill, giving up her black cow, Mora; and from now on their two sheds were sad and empty.

This was also a sad moment for us as the twice daily visits to Rina to get the milk, hear all the latest news, and have a few words with Signora Maria and Tranquillo were now much reduced as we couldn't continue to visit them twice a day without any excuse for doing so. Another result of the reduction in the number of quadrupeds in the area – mules, horses and cows – was that it became almost impossible to find real manure.

What was now very noticeable, with the discovery of television by the *contadini*, was the decline in conversation. At meal times people previously noted for their animation and powers of repartee could be seen trying to keep one eye on their plates and the other on the screen.

Now most families had cars and there were far fewer people passing our front door, such as Anselmo, fortified with *grappa*, shooting up the hill beyond the torrent on his way to his Monday morning shave, although we still had our daily visits from Orfeo and his wife, Maria, and Signor Giuseppe and Signora Fernanda and also Franca, Nino's wife. As people walked less, the footpaths gradually became overgrown and forgotten.

By now, people from Sarzana and further afield were beginning to build houses up the hill along the road from Caniparola to Fosdinovo – some of them pseudo-Alpine constructions which looked a bit odd. Their owners surrounded them with high metal fences which, now that no one walked anywhere any more, were often erected across rights-of-way (a subject in which we were no longer interested), without anyone protesting. Within these enclosures, which had electrically operated gates, savage guard dogs roamed untethered. The hillside was rapidly becoming suburbanized, as Caniparola and other such places down in the plain had already been long since. At the Festa di San Remigio the drinking booths with the long tables at which the farmers sat eating and drinking had disappeared a long time ago, although the midday meal at the hotel in Fosdinovo where Wanda had worked as a waitress for so many years was still served.

Now children were going to Elba and Sardinia on holiday, and wearing bikinis. None of the men, except the aged ones, wore suits when working in the fields any more. No one grew wheat. What really held the rural life in one piece was the *vendemmia* and the harvesting of the olives, both of which still had to be done by hand.

And for us there was the problem of I Castagni. Every autumn after the *vendemmia* we used to set off for England, returning the following spring, leaving the vines and the olives in the hands of Signor Giuseppe, who continued to do the work of pruning the vines, racking the wine during the winter, spraying the grapes throughout the summer and doing all the other work that was necessary, except digging and manuring, jobs that were in my province. And even so I subsequently hired a tractor to do the digging, having discovered that to do something by hand when you can find a machine to do it is just sentimental nonsense. I had already employed one long before this to make a new *vigneto* after the gargantuan efforts Attilio and I had made in digging the first one.

Then one day Signor Giuseppe intimated that he felt that he could no longer continue the task of looking after our *vigneto* and pruning and spraying the vines and harvesting the olives any more; and Signora Fernanda said '*mosca!*' several times in succession, something we had never heard her do before. She was very sad. Signor Orfeo from up the hill offered to carry on with the work and did for a time but we finally decided, with terrible heart-searchings, to give up. There is a time in everyone's life to leave a place, however much you love it, and this was it.

We finally left I Castagni in the winter of 1991. The pleasure of having lived in it all those years and meeting all those people who had become associated with it, the survivors of whom we now had to bid farewell to, was incalculable.

As they always had been, the farewells were said the previous evening, and as always we left the following morning before anyone else was up and about, that is except for Rina whose years milking Bionda at this time of day had made it impossible for her to rid herself of the habit of getting up at first light, and Tranquillo who was already far away with his tractor and trailer in the woods.

As usual when anything of importance happened at I Castagni it was pouring with rain and the last memory we had of it when we turned to look down on it was rather a sad one, of something we had lost for ever.

It has taken us a long time even to begin to realize that we aren't part of the life of I Castagni any more, and I don't think we ever will realize it completely as long as we live.

THE LONELY PLANET STORY

Where it all began…

A beat-up old car, a few dollars in the pocket, and a sense of adventure.

That's all Tony and Maureen Wheeler needed for the trip of a lifetime. They met on a park bench in Regent's Park and married a year later. For their honeymoon, they decided to attempt what few people thought possible – crossing Europe and Asia overland, all the way to Australia. It took them several months and all the money they could earn, beg or borrow, but they made it. And at the end of it all, they were flat broke… and couldn't have been happier.

It was too amazing an experience to keep to themselves. Urged on by their friends, they stayed up nights at their kitchen table writing, typing and stapling together their very first travel guide, Across Asia on the Cheap.

Within a week they'd sold 1500 copies and Lonely Planet was born. Two years later, their second journey led to South-East Asia on a shoestring, which led to books on Nepal, Australia, Africa, and India, which led to… you get the picture.

Fast-forward over 30 years.

As Lonely Planet became a globally loved brand, Tony and Maureen received several offers for the company. But it wasn't until 2007 that they found a partner whom they trusted to remain true to Lonely Planet's principles. In October of that year, BBC Worldwide acquired a 75% share in Lonely Planet, pledging to uphold Lonely Planet's commitment to independent travel, trustworthy advice and editorial independence.

BBC Worldwide is the main commercial arm, and a wholly owned subsidiary of, the British Broadcasting Corporation (BBC).

Today, Lonely Planet has offices in Melbourne, London and Oakland, with over 500 staff members and 300 authors. Tony and Maureen are still actively involved with Lonely Planet. They're travelling more often than ever, and they're devoting their spare time to charitable projects. And the company is still driven by the philosophy in Across Asia on the Cheap: 'All you've got to do is decide to go and the hardest part is over. So go!'